Electric Ecosystem

Everytl by elec and m(

The hope is that this book inspires and confronts. It takes you on a journey through a world in which humans, animals and plants all appear to be speaking the language of electrical signals.

In a scientific anecdotal way, pieces of the puzzle are fitted together into a wonderful and at the same time reflective whole that calls for contemplation and dialogue about the vulnerability of the ecosystem in which truly everything turns out to be electrically connected in a mysterious way, and in which even the most silent frequencies can bring about the greatest changes.

Bacteria appear to communicate by 'mobile phones', migratory birds 'google' the best bird restaurants and frogs float on invisible magnetic fields. Chapter by chapter, the amazement grows when you read that not only bees, trees, cells, cats, hummingbirds, garden cress, clouds and zebra fish have all kinds of electrical characteristics, but so do solar systems and galaxies.

All in all, this natural electric influence is such that now, with the arrival of new wireless techniques and frequencies, more and more questions are arising about the safety of the electric ecosystem.

Electric Ecosystem

Everything works by electricity and magnetism

Context Serie

Layout and design
Lydia Funneman, Pit Ontwerp, Nijmegen, Netherlands

Cover
Mark Stolk, den Malende Hollaender, Denmark

Black-and-white illustrations
Sander Funneman

Editing
Gerda van Schaik

Editing and advice
Anne-Marie Meevis

English translation, editing and advice
Lianne Wouters, Focus Vertalingen, Netherlands
Anna Hannon, United Kingdom
Rosamond Rolleston, United Kingdom

www.electric-ecosystem.com

The scientific researches quoted in this book have been compiled as completely as possible in the list of references.

This publication assumes that the reader is aware that the author's ideas are philosophical until such time as sufficient evidence has been gathered to accept these as fact.

For a liveable future.
For the generations to come.
For Davin, Niekan, Winsten, Kimia and Rowin.

Contents

Introduction |

With this research project, I have become more aware than ever of the omnipresence of ecosystems: the universe is an ecosystem, the solar system is an ecosystem, the planetary environment is an ecosystem, a forest is an ecosystem, a national state is an ecosystem, a park, a lake, a pond and a garden are ecosystems.

In general, ecosystems are: (1) coherent networks of relationships between organisms, (2) with a circulation of matter where one organism's waste is another's food, resulting in a system in which raw materials and energy are never exhausted, (3) in which exists a dynamic balance with room for evolution and (4) with a self-repairing, resilient capacity which allows for the absorption of disturbances. But, is this really complete? What if this is just the physical foundation of something with many more levels?

This research project started in the summer of 1986. After a lecture in a small hall of 'De Vereeniging', a concert hall in Nijmegen, The Netherlands, my wife and I were given a hand-out in English. The text revolved around energy and introduced the idea that 'Everything works by electricity and magnetism'. If it had said 'Some things seem to work by electricity and magnetism' we would probably have overlooked it, but 'everything', well... This definitive statement caused a reaction in us, the feeling a blunt knife must have when it spots a whetstone. We wanted to be able to refute this completely, but at the same time there was an irresistible urge to gather information so that it could be irrefutably substantiated. The mind registered a slight shimmer in the air and an opportunity to sharpen itself.

This marked interest was also fuelled by subsequent personal experiences.

If maybe there are seven levels that could describe this research project, then this book is a first beginning of level 1. It is a level 1 book with the hope and the vision that possibly all seven levels will see the light of day at some point, in any form whatsoever. After all, most of these levels are not suitable for a book; they manifest themselves in applications, experiences, theatre and life-centering stories. The first level's advantage over all other levels is that as many facts and references as possible are provided in raw form. These are open to individual interpretation, rearrangement, reflection and a personal search for the other levels. You can do with it whatever you want. For the sake of readability, it was decided to introduce some structure. That structure limits itself to arranging bees with bees, frogs with frogs, cells with cells and birds with birds. This structure is kept to a minimum, so that the references might easily be rearranged at higher levels.

Now, in this day and age, electricity and magnetism can be immediately googled in all kinds of variants. This was not yet possible in 1986. There was no internet. We did not even have a decent encyclopaedia. Our source was the library.

The perception that everything works by electricity and magnetism made a deep impression and grabbed our attention from then on. It has taken us into a world in which everything does, in fact, fundamentally appear to work by means of electricity and magnetism. At the same time this perception clashed with everything we had learned so far. This idea felt new and exciting, but also turned the world upside down. "What do you mean, 'everything'?" Does that mean that human behaviour and human individuality also work on the basis of electricity and magnetism? It is clear that the heart, the nerves and the brain have certain electrical characteristics. But does that also apply to muscles, the way bees fly from one flower to another, how bacteria form a biofilm, how birds navigate, how embryos grow, and plants communicate? What about the way in which all chemical substances in our bodies work? And what about the gravity in which it is precisely mass that keeps the planets in an orbit around the sun - does it also work by electricity and magnetism? Because all those questions could not be googled at the time, we decided to dedicate a food box to the subject. It was an orange box once used for gherkin jars and it was made of an uncommonly sturdy type of cardboard. In fact, the box still smelled a bit like gherkins, but it fitted nicely under the bed.

That box slowly started to be filled with clues. Of course, first of all an obvious reference about the method of measuring the electrical activity of the brain, the EEG, was put in. My parents once had an EEG performed of my head when it was hit by the crossbar of a goalpost. Next, a reference was added about the way potato plants grow into much larger plants with bigger potatoes under the influence of a strong magnetic field [1]. And then there was a reference about the fact that a raindrop's electric charge increases as clouds warm up [2]. A photocopy from a booklet found in a bookstore in Cambridge, England, investigating the way bacteria react to the earth's magnetic field was also put in [3]. The owner of the bookstore was kind enough to make a copy in his office behind the shop. As the gherkin box became increasingly filled with newspaper clippings, pictures and copies in the 1990s, the smell of gherkins gradually disappeared. It was replaced by the somewhat musty smell of old paper. By now, much had been collected in all manner of areas. Somewhere halfway through the 1990s, an article about the technique for also measuring the brain's magnetic fields, the MEG, was a new highlight. This completed the circle and brought the research project much closer to home because it turned out that the brain is full of measurable electrical activity and also generates a magnetic field. So, this was happily popped into the gherkin box. I remember how this last reference brought a sense of inspiration, because it confirmed Maxwell's law which says that an electric current cannot exist without a magnetic field. From that moment on, this law no longer only applied to the electricity that travelled through the wires in the walls, but also to the electricity in heads.

Such insights led to the temptation to formulate theories, but although this book shares fragments of theory, it has been deliberately decided to avoid the formation of theories as much as possible at this stage of presentation. In short, this book does not aim to draw conclusions, but to use the contents of the gherkin box to ask a few important, fundamental questions. The references and the facts speak for themselves and could lead to more research and process.

The collector's bug started to have its effect and gradually began to change our way of looking at things. The idea of an ecosystem in which only the circulation of matter is important and in which one organism's waste is another's food, started to be overturned. We started to see how the causal role of energy in the ecosystem had been underexposed. In 1986, it was known that the heart and the head work by means of electrical signals, but the magnetic fields were nowhere to be seen. They could not yet be measured, and the general assumption was that they therefore would not exist anyway. New insights were formed. In addition to the method of measuring the electrical currents of the heart, i.e. the ECG, ways were also developed to measure the magnetic field of the heart, i.e. the MCG.

Everyone knows that the brain does not consist of a single

lobe, but of two lobes. The left and right halves of the brain each have their own nature. Could it be that one half is more magnetic and the other one more electric? It would take until 2012 before neurologists published a research in the journal 'Brain' on how, by brain stimulation, a general magnetic influence can be exerted which has a mediating effect on the, sometimes conflicting, processes between the two halves of the brain. There are a number of reasons why people have less regard for processes in one of the two halves of the brain. This phenomenon is called neglect and can result in people, for example, only eating half their plate of carrots because half of the plate remains invisible to them. This can be overcome by magnetic stimulation. Researchers know it works, but why it works and how long it works is unknown [4*].

While our very first computer entered the house as early as 1989, it took well into the new millennium before the gherkin box transformed into a digital folder on the computer. Once the folder had become a folder structure, the box eventually disappeared into rubbish bin.

The beauty of something that is actually true is that it can take you further and further into the mystery of that truth. This is how we discovered there are levels to the understanding that everything works by electricity and magnetism. In her beautiful book, 'The Spark of Life', Frances Ashcroft describes the fundamental difference between the electricity energizing the bodies of people and animals and the electricity we use to light our cities at night. The electricity in the wiring inside the walls is carried by fast electrons, while the slow electricity that runs through the animal kingdom is carried by ions. An electric signal through a wire travels almost at the speed of light, i.e. 300,000 kilometres per second, while the fastest nerve impulses travel at about 0.12 kilometres per second [5*].

As previously stated, this book will not deal with the way all kinds of theories regarding electricity and magnetism relate to each other. It is mainly about the practicality of things in the ecosystem and about the scientific anecdotes illustrating that all life is not just made up of substances and chemistry, but is animated by energy, impulses and radiation frequencies. This book is far from complete. In fact, it is our feeling that, after more than 30 years of research, the discoveries in this field have only just begun. Turning a way of thinking that holds on to the thought that everything works by physical chemical processes into the understanding that electromagnetism affects life in many more different ways than we think, still has a long way to go.

In every research, there will be times when experiences begin to catch up with the theory of the research. In 2006 we came across a reference that made us pay more attention to solar activities. It was a 1987 research that established a direct link between migraine episodes and geomagnetic activity [6*]. To our surprise, we also discovered a connection between headache symptoms and geomagnetic activities.

In 2002 we came across an article by cardiologist Eliyahu Stoupel. He had observed that all people are sensitive to the natural variations in the magnetic field around the earth, but heart patients seem to be particularly sensitive to them. Stoupel stated that he had plotted the geomagnetic activities on a scale which he subdivided into four gradations: quiet, unstable, active and stormy. Over a period of twenty years he had linked the medical records of his patients and the examination reports of healthy blood donors to the geomagnetic activities prevailing at the time. His research showed that on days with active or stormy geomagnetic activity significantly more heart attacks and strokes occured than on other days. On those days, the average blood pressure was higher, while the risk of clot formation also increased. During his research, he was also able to confirm the 1987 finding of the link between migraine attacks in people suffering from it, and stormy geomagnetic activities [7*, 8*].

Imagine a huge jigsaw of 10,000 pieces scattered on a large table. The puzzle pieces together constitute the electric ecosystem: how the cells use electrical signals, how clouds emit electrical frequencies, how plants emit electromagnetic messages to bees, and how elephant nose fish talk to each other in an electromagnetic dialect. There is no lid on this jigsaw puzzle box, so there is no example of what the finished jigsaw would look like. There are just 10,000 loose pieces. Fitting these pieces together will create an image of the integrated electric ecosystem and may allow for understanding of many natural phenomena, such as the coordination inside a flight of starlings, the way in which a colony of bacteria is able to jointly form into a bacteria city with beautiful architectural shapes, or the logic behind the way trees electrically charge the air above forests. This book will show that a lot of things that happen between trees and plants, between animals and the earth's magnetic field and between cells themselves, cannot be understood without involving the influence of electrical signals.

But now imagine that, while those 10,000 pieces are on the table, someone enters and quickly mixes in 100 pieces that do not fit. Those 100 pieces are not part of the natural electric ecosystem but symbolize the artificial frequencies. Increasingly often, new artificial pieces are secretly put on the table without anyone even noticing it. This has changed the puzzle.

This research project will initially start by laying out the magic puzzle of the natural electric ecosystem. It does not aim for an end result. It opens up an area of related questions that invite a process: what kind of electrical exchanges take place naturally in a forest, in a school of fish, between a predator and its prey, between insects themselves? And what are the electromagnetic exchanges in a much larger context between planets, the solar system and galaxies?

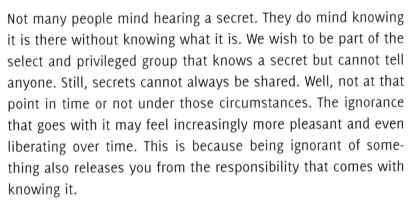

Animals, Plants and the Earth

How plants and animals do not live on but in a smart planet and how they use the intelligent 'internet of things' of that planet without hmans knowing anything about it

Not many people mind hearing a secret. They do mind knowing it is there without knowing what it is. We wish to be part of the select and privileged group that knows a secret but cannot tell anyone. Still, secrets cannot always be shared. Well, not at that point in time or not under those circumstances. The ignorance that goes with it may feel increasingly more pleasant and even liberating over time. This is because being ignorant of something also releases you from the responsibility that comes with knowing it.

Trees know it. Trees intercommunicate by means of electrical impulses. Bleep, bleep, bleep... They use their roots to exchange signals with other trees and their surroundings at a speed of one centimetre per second. Plants have memories and are capable of learning things. They appear to be highly sensitive and deal intelligently with their surroundings. The root system of trees can be compared to a gigantic brain system that functions as a root wide web, an internet used by trees to exchange information by means of electromagnetic signals [1*]. The same is true for the exchange of substances, which is dealt with in other books.

But there is more. Worms, too, communicate with each other by means of the same slow, electrical impulses that reach, inform, alert or support their own species through the ground. Jellyfish do so by using the saltwater [2*].

Most and possibly all forms of life on earth take part in

this secret and make use of all its exclusive benefits. However, almost the entire human world population has no idea about it whatsoever. We are born, live and die without ever having had a clue. How can that be? How is this possible with all our technical ingenuity?

Maybe nobody wants to know the secret. Maybe it would wreak too much havoc on our culture with all its systems, classes and orders. Still, it is precisely the curiosity for the unknown that is the basis of every new system and every new order. It is precisely that deep desire to unearth secrets from nature and become initiated into the enigmas of the as yet unseen worlds around us that continues to bring us new perceptions.

For Linnaeus, life was one great voyage of discovery. He started his work as a biologist by taking a fresh look at things. He looked at nature as if he saw it for the first time. He studied plant forms and counted stamens and started to classify plants according to their reproductive organs. Carolus Linnaeus (1707-1778) was a Swedish physician and botanist who was the first to develop a system to classify plants. He was born the son of Nils and Christiana. As was common in those days, his father did not have a family name but needed one when the still young Nils went to study. When choosing the family name, he let himself be inspired by the giant linden tree near to the house where he was born, the name of which he Latinised into Linnaeus. And this was the family name from then on. In 1735, Carolus Linnaeus published his main work, Systema Naturae, the system of nature through the three kingdoms of nature, according to classes, orders, genera and species, with characters, differences, synonyms and places. He described the three natural kingdoms of animals, plants and minerals. The sexual nature of his classification and the use of sexual terminology, very explicit at the time, made the system controversial for his contemporaries.

He took the liberty of developing an entirely new system that is still in use worldwide today.

Linnaeus himself was not bothered by the definitions he created. We, however, are. The deeper we delve into the nomenclature of animals, plants and minerals, the less we see. The secret squirrels share with geckos, spiders, lobsters and lesser capricorn beetles becomes more and more removed from our abilities to participate. Is it not true that looking at something with a fresh pair of eyes is forgotten once you know its name?

Imagine two squirrels nudging each other in a back yard, exchanging a pitying look and, as they peek through the living room window where the humans are stuck in their ignorance, elsewhere two geckos run across the water. Naturally, squirrels and geckos are not aware of what they know, but they do use the intelligence and skills associated with the secret. The powers from that secret world allow geckos to run like lightning across a smooth surface, such as a glass window or a lake. Thanks to micro hairs on the bottom of their fingers and toes, geckos produce magical power. The hairs are so finely branched that the electrons in the ends exert a Van der Waals force on the surface molecules. The Van der Waals force is the weak electromagnetic force that exists between molecules [3*]. The Helmeted basilisk, or Jesus Christ lizard, also makes use of this electromagnetic force to walk on water. In addition, there are other animals with similar enigmatic abilities. For example, spiders, lobsters, millipedes and arthropods that not only anchor their orientation towards the earth's magnetic field and their magnetic senses in crystals in their bodies, but which have also imbedded this ability into their molecular structure [4*]. And then there is the great capricorn beetle, which is also influenced by magnetic fields in many ways [5*]. It is everywhere.

While we humans fill our consciousness with names and

identification, classification and categorisation, we miss the connection. We use Linnaeus' systems, but no longer observe like Linnaeus did. We do not even notice that electricity has a growth-stimulating effect on our bones [6*]; nor do we notice that fractured bones heal more quickly when exposed to the same frequencies which cats use to purr. Cats purr at frequencies between 25 and 150 Hertz, which are precisely the frequencies that cause fractured bones to heal more quickly when they are regularly exposed to those frequencies during recovery [7*]. Why is this the case?

Because it takes time to get our eyes used to things they have never seen before, here begins a sequence of descriptions of seemingly familiar life forms with whom we share this planet and which we, in essence, hardly understand.

Bees

How high-tech bees and wasps use smartphones, GPS and other gadgets

Of course there have been thousands of moments when everybody could have suddenly woken up. Moments when a window of opportunity opened and there was a glimpse of something that could have activated a strange new consciousness. Questions could have been asked and culture would have changed dramatically. But there it is…

When, in 2007, Ryan Ferguson bought his new house in Bath, England, he encountered a major problem: he discovered 30 bees' nests in the attic. The bees were everywhere and constituted a danger to him and his family. Twice he called the pest control service, but the bees kept coming back. Then he installed his Wi-Fi system, with a good overall range in the house and in the attic. Instantly, the bees disappeared never to return [1*].

High-tech bees and wasps with smart nests

A genius bee technology is the hexagonal honeycomb made of beeswax. This beeswax, used for making the honeycomb architecture, is secreted by worker bees during a certain phase of life. The honeycomb shape is brilliant. Humans have copied this design and used it for various technical applications. The hexagonal shape of honeycombs is used by bees across the earth. This shape is indescribably robust and requires less material than any other shape. This is crucial, for the production of beeswax uses up honey. One bee needs five grams of honey to produce just one single gram of wax, and it takes eight bees all their working lives to make one single spoonful of honey. To do so, a bee has flown no less than 800 kilometres and made tens of thousands of intermediate stops. Just think about the amount of work and the life they live. For us humans, who sometimes casually drop a few scoops of honey in our tea, knowing this creates the possibility of converting our knowledge about the dedicated lives of bees into appreciation. By tasting the honey in our tea, we connect with the life's work of eight bees.

Wasps seem to find their way home by both mini crystals in their bodies and in the cells of their nests [2*]. The Oriental hornet is a species of wasp three times the size of wasps in the Netherlands and is found in the region between Turkey and Sudan. The inside of the hexagonal cells in their nests is fitted with an oval-shaped crystal. These crystals consist of the mineral titanium iron, or ilmenite, and therefore have a different composition to the rest of the nest. The purpose of the crystals is that the wasps, by means of electromagnetic signal transference (EMST), tune in to their specific crystal in the nest and are also guided by it when building the nest. The crystals inside the nest seem also to enable them to exchange information with the earth's magnetic field and to communicate with each other. So, they are true high-tech wasps with mobile phones in smart nests. How exactly wasps are guided by the crystals is still completely unknown. It is suspected that the insects themselves also carry a magnetic crystal as a kind of advanced mobile phone which they use to maintain that contact with each other, their nest and the geomagnetic field. The crystals in the nest, the crystals in the wasp and the geomagnetic field seem to relate to each other as an internet-connected Wi-Fi point and an iPad. Humans have only recently become aware of these advanced technologies in nature, hardly any research has been done into the frequencies wasps and bees use to communicate. The whole area of EMST in nature is still unexplored territory.

The relationship between humans and bees is thousands of years old. In ancient Egypt, about 6,000 years ago, the first beekeepers kept their bees in ceramic tubes. These tubes had a length of about one metre and a diameter of 25 centimetres. Both ends were sealed with a cap. One of the two caps had an opening through which the bees could enter and leave the tubes. These tubes were stacked horizontally and entire walls were created in this way. The Egyptians knew that they could use smoke to calm the bees. For many millennia now, humans have known what bees are capable of and how they can use them for the production of honey. But what did humans learn in all this time about the hidden life of bees? It is almost unimaginable that wasps and bees, at a time when humans still roamed the forests carrying clubs, already phoned each other, maintained wireless contact with their smart nests and were able to navigate on the earth's magnetic field.

 ## Positively charged bees and negatively charged flowers

Bees have been doing their work in the same social forms for millions of years. They originate from Asia and arrived in Europe about 300,000 years ago. The only species of bees still living in Northern Europe is *Apis mellifera*. For many thousands of years now, the lives of these insects have been intertwined with the lives of humans. Humans have been keeping bees since ancient times. Ancient Egypt pharaohs saw them as something divine, as tears of the sun god and as miracles of creation. In the centuries that followed, that way of looking at these insects began to decay. Now, from an economic point of view, they are merely workers. In today's world, honeybees are the third most important working animals, after cows and pigs, as they pollinate 80 percent of wild plants and crops, ranging from apples, pears, rapeseed, peaches and raspberries to clover, linseed, beans, peas and cucumbers. It should also be noted that the yield of the harvest is in many cases much higher if bees are responsible for pollination. So why is pollination by bees so hugely effective? The answer to this question is only just beginning to be formulated.

In the 1980s, scientists discovered that the electromagnetic charges carried by bees could amount to hundreds of volts [3*]. A bee flaps its wings 250 times per second and the electromagnetic charge increases with every wing beat. They are, in fact, flying storage batteries. Even though there was a suspicion in those years that the electromagnetic charges in honeybees serve an important ecological purpose, this purpose remained unseen until, in 2013, well over 30 years later. It then became apparent that not only bees do by nature collect electromagnetic charges when they fly [4*], but that flowers, rooted in soil, in turn build up an electromagnetic charge when they gently sway in the wind. It has become evident that bees and flowers live together in an integrated world of electromagnetic interaction. The 2013 study revealed the magnificent ways in which all bees communicate by means of EMST: radiation, frequencies and impulses. Honeybees apparently communicate in a number of different electromagnetic dialects, both among each other and with plants. In fact, both plants and bees have an electric glow that is invisible to humans. When radiating that glow, plants emit weak, negatively charged electric fields, whereas bees become positively charged when they fly through the air, flapping their wings up and down at high speed. We now know that flowers radiate all kinds of electrical signal patterns. Bees are able to distinguish these different floral frequencies, using electroreception [5*]. Bees are therefore involved in some form of plant identification, not by counting the stamens like Linnaeus did, but by scanning the electromagnetic signature of plants with their inbuilt 'smartphones'. They do not classify plants according to language or Latin names, but according to electromagnetic spectral frequencies. How do these electromagnetic charges between flowers and bees develop? Well, by polarisation. This involves four ingredients: bees, flowers, the planet and the electromagnetic field of the earth. The electromagnetic charges between flowers and bees are caused as follows: the positively charged atmospheric electromagnetic field of the earth ensures that the bees too become positively charged and the earth itself is negatively charged, so that plants also build up a negative charge [6*].

Pollination by electromagnetic discharge and why bumblebees can fly

The geospheric circuit generates a permanent electromagnetic charge between the earth's surface and the higher atmosphere [7*]. The ground and the plants linked to it are negatively charged [8*], whereas birds, bees and other flying insects build up a positive charge as they are in contact with air molecules [9*]. Electric charges emanating from plants (negative) and pollinators, such as bees (positive), are believed to promote pollination by enabling pollen grains to jump from the flowers to the pollinators and vice versa [3*]. Two recent studies reveal that bees can not only detect these electric fields but are also able to distinguish all kinds of other fields with various frequencies. This makes electroreception a very serious matter in the world of animals [10*].

Bumblebees, the larger and somewhat fluffier species of bees, are better able to withstand cold because of their thick fur and can therefore live as far north as the Arctic Circle. But based on the laws of aerodynamics, they are too heavy to keep themselves afloat with their small wings. One theory states that bumblebees can fly because they move their wings in a special way, such that they generate adequate electromagnetic charge to allow them to use the forces in the earth's magnetic field to stay afloat. Naturally, this requires further investigation. Like common bees, bumblebees recognize floral frequencies through electroreception. The electromagnetic field of a flower tells them whether a visit is worth their while. It further appears that honeybees are attracted to assembly points in the air that have a specific electromagnetic signature [11*].

Bees speak in
dance frequencies

It is the pollination activities of bees that ensure that we, in principle, have enough food at our disposal and can enjoy its enormous diversity. The beekeepers from ancient Egypt built ships for their beehives and sailed along the Nile up to the estuary of the Mediterranean Sea throughout the season. That way they could benefit from the differences in flowering time between inland and coast. Over time, they learned to sail only at night, because the bees could not retrace the hive when it had been moved during the day. If they moved a bee colony at night, the bees reoriented themselves the next day and effortlessly found their way back to the hive. Like the Egyptians, the ancient Greeks also regarded the honeybee initially as divine. Artemis, the Ephesian goddess of fertility, was depicted with these insects. Her priestesses were called Melissae after 'melissa', the Greek word for honeybee. The great cultural amazement about the existence of the bee disappeared in the same period as when people discovered how exceptionally useful a bee colony could be. The economic imperative became a pair of glasses through which people started to look at nature, and this perspective deprived the honeybee of its existence as an independent form of life. Economic thinking only attached value to benefit, production, yield and profit. The divine glow surrounding the bee colony, perceived by the ancient Greeks, faded away; more precisely, the glow of bees faded away in the eyes of humans. The bees themselves, however, have not paid one iota of attention to the fact that people lost their metaphysical view of the bee colony.

In the centuries after the ancient Greeks, people started to look more and more at the way bees danced, without 'seeing it', without kindling a spark, but from an economic point of view. All kinds of characteristics were mapped out about the round dance, the sickle dance, the waggle dance and the vibration dance which bees use to give each other directions about food and potential nesting places. Beekeepers were able to derive all kinds of useful information from studying the bee dance. Only in 1980 was it established that this dance, so typical of bees, is also controlled and influenced by the earth's magnetic field. Even demagnetised bees were still able to orientate on the earth's magnetic field using EMST. This meant that bees possessed other magnetic powers, undetectable by humans at that time [12*]. Researchers did measure that the electromagnetic signals generated by bees whilst dancing had a frequency between 180 and 250 Hz[13*]. These frequencies sensitise bees to the radiation of power pylons which causes them pain. Frequencies in the range of 30 KHz – 300 GHz appear to disturb the bee dance [14*]. Further research on the subject is needed.

Bees send and receive messages with their antennae

Today, 70 out of 100 plant species, which account for more than 90 percent of the human diet, are pollinated by bees. The economic life of humans would be inconceivable without the honeybee. In spite of this, their existence is under threat. The greatest threat is posed by the lack of knowledge about the electromagnetic life of bees. There is so much we can learn from bees and wasps. The knowledge about their economic significance for us is vast, but there are few tools to understand their life in the way they experience it themselves. It is said that we should take every possible measure to keep bees protected and healthy so they can continue doing their important work. This gives, however, no consideration to the fact that bees also require space and time to do the things they have to do without any relevance to human beings. If we cannot allow bees and other animals to be themselves, how can we expect them to continue to give the fruits of their labour?

The antennae of bees also have electrical functions. The presence of electrical charges during their annual cycle is significant. Moreover, electrical influences seem to help explain some aspects of bee-parasite relationships [15*]. All kinds of insects also appear to build up and exchange a multitude of electrical charges via their antennae in social interactions with each other and their surroundings. The meaning of the language of frequencies that animals use for this is unknown and the scope of the exchanges between species, the whole ecosystem and the earth's magnetic field is also unknown. Yet more and more artificially generated signals in ever higher frequencies are being emitted into the air. The whole ecosystem is bombarded with unimaginable amounts of electromagnetic frequencies that generate a thick soup of electrosmog covering the earth. The ingredients of that electric soup are becoming increasingly complex in nature. Nobody knows how this affects bees' antennae. No research has been done as yet. If we were to know now what the growing understanding of the influence of wireless communication on bees could tell us, would we make different choices? If we were to know that bees fall ill as a result of Wi-Fi or experience pain when exposed to radiation from transmission masts, would we then put ecological interests before economic interests?

In 2018, the Swiss organisation Pro Natura published the results of a study into the effects of radiation from transmission masts on insects. Their study shows that insects are best able to absorb radiation at frequencies equal to or smaller than their body size. Electromagnetic frequencies above 6 GHz are best absorbed by insects. A shift of 10% of the radiation energy to frequencies above 6 GHz leads to an increase in absorbed power between 3-370%. The result: changes in insect behaviour, changes in physiology and in morphology. The next generation of wireless technology is expected to operate at those frequencies above 6 GHz [16*].

 ## Navigating on the earth's magnetic field using the magnetic sense

After the ancient Egyptians and ancient Greeks, the ancient Roman church fathers started seeing the honeybee not as a divine form of life, but as a source for their analogies. As an example, they saw the bee colony as the ideal model for a monastic community. Theologians considered the queen bee a symbol for the virginity of Mary, because they did not know at that time that the queen of a bee colony can lay about 2,000 fertilized eggs a day for years. In order for her to lay so many fertilized eggs on a daily basis, her attendants, consisting of 12 worker bees, provide her with superfood, called royal jelly. Just like the ancient church fathers, we constantly have to adjust our image of the bees, too. Again and again we have to take account of new insights. The fact that the antennae of various animals are capable of sending and receiving electromagnetic signals is still not commonly accepted knowledge. Had this indeed become part of our collective consciousness, we would perhaps now be more careful with wireless communication.

The abdomen of honeybees contains a space filled with magnetite crystals, iron oxide particles that can register changes in the earth's magnetic field [17*, 18*, 19*, 20*]. By now, this magnetic sense has also been observed in many other animals, such as dolphins, ants, lobsters, butterflies, flatworms, bacteria and spiders. In pigeons, for instance, a densely innervated spot in the skull has been found which contains biological magnetite. But what do animals use it for? What functions does it fulfil? We now know from a growing body of research that a number of animals navigate on the earth's magnetic field by using their magnetic sense. Initially, it was assumed that this was the only use for that sense and that many animals have an in-built sat-nav that helps them orientate. But it soon became clear that bees with that special sense could, for example, also orient building their honeycombs on the earth's magnetic field [21*]. It turned out they navigate and orientate on the earth's magnetic field and communicate with it. They extract much more information from it than we humans could ever have imagined. Well, this is necessary when you consider that one beehive can house as many as 50,000 bees, all of which must be able to do their work without hindering each other. The more the secrets of the EMST reveal themselves, the more we may realise whilst listening to the busy hum in the garden, that bees might look up to us from their diligent work to shake their heads pityingly over so little natural electromagnetic connection. Their lives are entangled with the 'natural internet of things'. Animals have been connected to it for thousands of years. We humans seem to have reached a crucial point now where sufficient scientific substantiation has accrued to enable us to acknowledge that the natural internet of things exists and thus acknowledge that the electric ecosystem exists. But another road may also be taken, one where every effort is made to set up an artificial internet of things, with all the consequences this might entail.

Consequences of artificial electromagnetic frequencies

With all the natural electromagnetic activities of bees, it seems relevant to ask questions about the consequences of generating so many new artificial electromagnetic signals - questions about safety, about the desirability in the long term and about possible damage to the ecosystem. What are acceptable risks we can take with the lives of bees that occupy such a prominent place in the ecosystem? What are the acceptable risks we can take with the lives of bees in a system where everything is interconnected? And before implementing new technology, how much patience can we muster to guarantee that the interests of one side do not lead to the irreversible downfall of another? Do we implement our technologies only because we can and because circumstances allow it? Or are we patiently searching for a deeper motivation and necessity? Economic impatience has led to thalidomide babies, ocean plastics and global warming. We know by now that acting out of ignorance may have disastrous consequences. Yet the economic temptation is strong. In retrospect, we would have promptly instituted a circular economy had we known before that a non-circular economy would prove to be so harmful. With all the collected insights and experiences you would expect us to be much more careful now with handling seemingly harmless new discoveries and possibilities. As long ago as the 1930s, not long after the electrification of the world, rumours about the negative influence of electromagnetic radiation started to emerge.

Bees, like all other animals and plants, lived in a natural conductive unity in the earth's electromagnetic field for thousands of years. They used EMST to communicate with each other, with the flowers and with the earth's magnetic field. Consequently, they were hit hard by the arrival of power pylons. Other examples of the possible impact of artificial EMFs on the natural functioning of bees can be found in the chapter on the consequences for animals and plants.

Humans can potentially do what bees do but fail to put it into action

Humans think they are outside the natural internet of things. But the earth provides that internet without access codes, without firewalls, without security systems, to all life, including human beings. However much humans see the world of bees and other animals as strange, incomprehensible forms of life, we have the same invitation to log on to the natural internet of things. For just like land animals, birds, fish and bacteria, humans can navigate on the earth's magnetic field by means of a crystal in their heads, but fail to put it into action (yet). This is described in detail in the chapter on humans. We know from the studies on the animal kingdom that this crystal has all kinds of intuitive and intelligent features.

Why are we not taught in school to develop that sense of

orientation? Why do we learn to play with a smartphone in our hands and not with the smartphone in our heads? How is it possible that these electromagnetic abilities have been used for thousands of years without any problem by billions of bees, wasps and almost all other animal species without humans knowing about it? How is it possible that this unseen world of frequencies and signals could unite and integrate almost all animals over and over again, connecting and directing them, without it being discovered by humans? How is it possible that bees and wasps were connected to an indivisible electromagnetic web of life that remained inspired, nourished, informed by and connected to the earth's magnetic field, while we humans for centuries just ate honey without seeing it, without feeling it or without having a single clue about the electromagnetic language that bees speak to each other?

High-tech bees

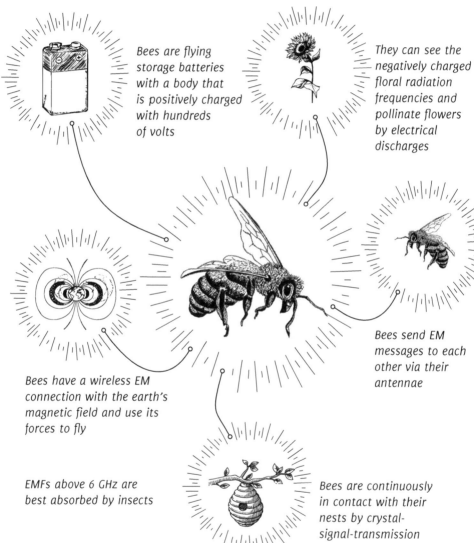

Bees make dance steps with which they transmit natural EM signals to each other, and are sensitive to artificial EMFs that disturb the dance steps

Artificial EMFs cause changes in bee behaviour, physiology and morphology

Bees are flying storage batteries with a body that is positively charged with hundreds of volts

They can see the negatively charged floral radiation frequencies and pollinate flowers by electrical discharges

Bees send EM messages to each other via their antennae

Bees have a wireless EM connection with the earth's magnetic field and use its forces to fly

EMFs above 6 GHz are best absorbed by insects

Bees are continuously in contact with their nests by crystal-signal-transmission

Bacteria

There is a lot of facebooking and twittering going on among animals. Various animal species form their own groups and share all kind of things. Contrary to the exchanges on the artificial internet, no trivia is exchanged. The natural internet, with the earth's magnetic field as its provider, has real meaning and purpose. That internet even allows animals to upload and download life energy via the websites of their species. This chapter aims to put the smallest of animals under the magnifying glass, i.e. bacteria and viruses.

At an early age, Antoni van Leeuwenhoek took a vivid interest in astronomy, maths, physics and chemistry. Nevertheless, he started working as a fabric merchant, which meant he had access to the best lenses of that time to examine purchased fabrics. In those days, microscopes had a magnifying power of 30, but when Van Leeuwenhoek began focusing his assembled lenses on other things besides fabrics, he developed a magnifying power of 270. The bacteria came into view.

First of all, bacteria and viruses produce electricity [1*, 2*, 3*]. These tiny forms of life, or "dierkens" as Van Leeuwenhoek called them, converted a huge variety of organic substances into pure electricity without the slightest difficulty. Antoni van Leeuwenhoek was completely unaware of this, because al-though he was the first man on earth to see a bacterium in 1676, at the time he could not have had any idea about the electromagnetic context in which bacteria live. No matter how powerful microscopes became in the following centuries, they would never be able to make that context visible. That required an entirely different way of looking.

The things that bring bacteria to life can also kill them

Some bacteria are completely annihilated under the influence of EMFs, while other microorganisms thrive under that same influence. Some EMFs cause bacteria and viruses to disappear like snow in summer, while others incite them to multiply massively. This is confirmed by a remarkable research into mould. A mould culture exposed to EMFs developed 600 times more biotoxins than a mould culture not exposed to EMFs [4]. The research also shows that EMFs within the GHz range can unleash retroviruses. In addition, milk products were exposed to EMFs of 129 GHz. The vital functions of lactic acid bacteria were investigated in three kinds of lactic acid products. The acidity in all three products reduced and the number of lactic acid bacteria increased [5]. Conversely, it appears that bacteria can be successfully annihilated by exposure to electromagnetic impulses. There is a research in which bacteria in a fluid were annihilated by means of high frequency electrical impulses [6] and a research in which electrical impulses assisted in wound healing by stopping bacterial growth [7]. Tests were carried out to see whether microorganisms could be killed by electricity in laboratory conditions, too. The result was that a low voltage was successfully used to eradicate two species: *Serratia marcescens* and *Micrococcus roseus* [8]. It proved even possible to develop a method for determining the exact electromagnetic frequency of 60 GHz for a specific virus species to be eliminated. The next step is to determine whether this resonance method also works for other more complex viruses and bacteria [9].

Looking at bacteria through fresh eyes all the time

Antoni van Leeuwenhoek was not a scientist. As stated, he was a Renaissance man who worked in fabrics. Even though he qualified as a bookkeeper in Amsterdam, he remained very curious about many areas. He would not let anything force him in one direction. He studied a great many things while working in his fabrics shop during the day. There he met a lot of clients, but no fellow researchers with whom to discuss his discoveries. He kept discovering new things until the day he died - for example, the previously unknown disease he suffered from when he was 90 years old. He described it in such detail that he eventually died from "Van Leeuwenhoek's disease". In the centuries after Van Leeuwenhoek we would penetrate deeper and deeper into the physical life of bacteria with our increasingly strong microscopes. Based on current estimates, the earth is home to one trillion species of microorganisms, though only 10 million species are known. Each bacterium has its own character, its own behaviour and its own ways. Since the first discovery of the tiny small world of bacterial colonies, the microscope was focused on ever smaller physical phenomena and ever more details in the sometimes bizarre world of microbes. Currently the largest bacterial species turns out to be *Thiomargarita namibiensis*, the sulphur eating giant bacteria. Its size is about 0.75 mm. The smallest bacterial species is *Rickettsia,* about 0.0001 mm. in size. If these two met, and *Rickettsia* would comparatively be 2 metres high, then *Thiomargarita* would stick 1,500 metres up in the air. That is nearly twice the height of the tallest building on earth. Although these two lifeforms live in totally different worlds, there may be a context in which they can communicate with each other. This is the point where reality becomes more exciting than fiction. It appears there are EM fields, frequencies and signals that can easily bridge the differences in size between these strange creatures.

Wireless and wired communication among bacteria

For some, the chapter on bacteria and viruses may be the most difficult one to grasp, but it may also be the most rewarding. More than any other aspect of the electrical ecosystem, the world of microorganisms shows in minute detail how versatile and extensively everything works by electricity and magnetism. Once the scales have fallen from one's eyes, a wonderful and magnificent world full of strange phenomena will be revealed.

How does a bacterial colony function? A bacterial colony can divide work. For instance, the outer microbes may defend against threats or breathe for the whole, whereas bacteria living in a colony at the bottom of a lake may specialize in finding or producing food for the whole colony. Bacteria appear to use electrically charged particles to organize and synchronize all their activities inside the colony. On occasion, the electrical exchanges are so powerful that biofilms use these to recruit new bacteria from the surrounding area and to negotiate with neighbouring biofilms for their mutual well-being. Like the neurons in the brain, bacteria use potassium ions to propagate electrical signals. They transfer these signals via thin tubes, or nanowires [10*]. Microbes communicate with each other and their surroundings by means of both wireless and wired electromagnetic signals. Chromosomes act as antennae with signals that travel through genetic circuits to produce species-specific frequencies. The bacterial transmission frequency is around 1 KHz. Different species of bacteria have different DNA lengths in their chromosomes. These lengths determine the frequency. Bacteria that transmit wirelessly are basically not very different from bacteria that do so using nanowires. By communicating using nanowires microbes can form closed networks. From an evolutionary point of view, wireless bacteria seem younger than bacteria that communicate using nanowires [11*].

The question is whether DNA from the cells of higher life forms, such as plants, animals and humans, also use electromagnetic signalling, and would this be wired or wireless? This might be food for further research.

How bacteria produce magnets and live in conjunction with the geomagnetic field

In 1975, scientists discovered that bacteria could navigate on the magnetic field of the earth. To their amazement, they found magnetite crystals inside the bodies of these small creatures, responsible for wireless interaction with the earth's magnetic field. They discovered two bacterial species: south-seeking and north-seeking bacteria. The north-seeking bacteria are the majority in the northern hemisphere, where they are especially found in river and sea sediments, whereas they are mainly found in surface waters in the southern hemisphere. South-seeking bacteria live in sediment and are the majority in the southern hemisphere, while they are mainly found in surface waters in the northern hemisphere. Near the magnetic equator, where the earth's magnetic field is pointing neither downward nor upward, the north-seeking and south-seeking bacteria are present in equal numbers [12*].

In 2005, the discovery was made that bacteria contain nano-compasses. Bacterial cells appear to be arranged into magnetosomes, building blocks for stable chains which they use for navigation. Around these chains, a miraculous filamentous structure was observed [13*]. When this was discovered, things started to take off. In 2008, it became known that bacteria were able to use these filamentous magnetosomes among others to google the geomagnetic field for the best food available in sea and river sediments. The magnetic crystals allow bacteria to effortlessly log on to geomagnetic internet food sites that provide precise information about direction, route and location [14*].

Just as there are many valuable, important and constructive bacteria, there are harmful ones. Not harmful in themselves, but harmful to humans, animals and plants. In 2017, a way was found to kill harmful bacteria by infecting them with a virus that had been exposed to a magnetic field [15*].

The research into bacteria reached its provisional peak in 2009 when the DNA of a specific bacterium was unravelled: *Desulfovibrio magneticus*. This microbe can produce ultra-small magnets itself. The iron used by this bacterium to produce its magnets is always crystal shaped. *Desulfovibrio magneticus* glues a circular layer around the iron crystals, creating a spherical shape also known as a magnetosome. *Desulfovibrio magneticus* lives completely in conjunction with the geomagnetic field. The spherical shapes it creates, which are then arranged into chains, seem to enable the geomagnetic field to control, inform, direct and program the bacterium in every conceivable way. The bacterium must therefore be viewed more as an instrument of the earth's magnetic field rather than an independent microbe that uses the geomagnetic field [16*]. This is where the first clues start to emerge that suggest that bacteria are, in fact, doubly integrated forms of life, part of their own intranet and living both individually and collectively with the entire biofilm in conjunction with the geomagnetic field, i.e. a bacterial intranet inside the geomagnetic internet.

We tend to view animals, plants and bacteria the way we view ourselves, as individuals, as separate beings with separate lives. But this is not the way bacteria live. Their destiny is not only entangled with each other, it is also entangled with the geomagnetic context in which they live. That context seems to carry the intelligence of the way in which a biofilm can take its sometimes absolutely breathtaking shape.

Picture of a bacterial colony forming a beautiful pattern, by Eshel Ben-Jacobs

So, bacteria are not much inspired by what they are themselves, nor by what they can accomplish as a colony, but instead by the geomagnetic field that prompts them how to behave both individually and collectively. Bacteria lead a planetary integrated existence and are prepared to give their lives for the beautiful shapes they collectively create, ordered from above. It is not inconceivable that bacterial colonies all over the world express their geomagnetic entanglement in exactly the same way. This, too, could be a reason for further research into the intelligence that possibly resides in the geomagnetic field and the way in which this also influences other animals in their reactions and their behaviour. This unconditional microorganism commitment to the magnetic field of the earth is, for instance, illustrated by the fact that some bacteria perform magnetic division besides cell division. How do some bacteria break these magnets in themselves in half? The answer to that is simple. The bacterium bends its internal magnets to weaken them, after which magnetic division can begin [17*].

In the stream of all these insights into the electromagnetic life of microorganisms, the idea therefore presents itself that bacteria are not so much independent beings but rather multi-integrated geomagnetic beings that, on instruction from the geomagnetic field, can form living electricity cables at the bottom of oceans and elsewhere.

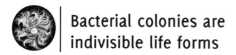 Bacterial colonies are indivisible life forms

Lars Peter Nielsen made another discovery about the *Desulfovibrio magneticus* microbe. The filamentous electric wires inside the bacterium simply continue outside the bacterium. Moreover, all bacteria together constitute a structure of filamentous electric wiring. Based on this, and on the interaction microbes have with the geomagnetic field, it is likely that the whole is essentially an indivisible organism that collectively is speaking one language, the language of electrical signals.

Soil samples for testing were collected from the Danish Bay of Aarhus. Nielsen noticed that more hydrogen sulphide was disappearing from the soil. The bacteria consumed the hydrogen sulphide. Ordinarily, they would require oxygen for this, but in the samples hydrogen sulphide was consumed in soil areas where there was no oxygen whatsoever. He did some more experiments and discovered an ingenious cooperation mechanism, because the bacteria in his samples had created a type of electrical grid between themselves. He realised that the bottom of the bay contained more than enough food, i.e. hydrogen sulphide, but little oxygen. The water surface shows a completely opposite picture. This is the reason why bacteria form long chains to convert oxygen and food into electrical signals and transport these signals from the bottom to the top, and vice versa. On the one hand, there are food-collecting bacteria and, on the other, oxygen-breathing bacteria. This ingenious cooperation mechanism, where food and oxygen are converted into electrical signals, enables the entire chain to live. In this way, bacteria help each other by means of the filamentous electric wires, giving them the energy they need. This also solved an existing mystery: why bacteria generate electricity [18*]. Would it not be incredibly easy if you never had to eat again but still got enough energy because a kindred spirit living on the edge of the city eats on your behalf?

All this leads to the remarkable conclusion that bacteria dwelling deeper into the soil consume for the entire community and that bacteria living on the water's surface breathe for the entire bacterial community. They can do so because the whole colony is interconnected and every action by the bacteria is translated and divided into electrical signals (EMST).

Nielsen must have looked out over the Bay of Aarhus at some point, realizing that it contained not just a couple of microbes scattered here and there but a giant living organism, a bacteroid larger than the largest dinosaur that ever lived, linking billions of microbes into an integrated life form: the *Desulfovibrio magneticus* mammoth that is inextricably linked to the geomagnetic field.

Bacteria as an extension of the geomagnetic field

Kenneth Nealson discovered all kinds of microbes that feed exclusively on pure electricity. The bacteria do not do this by conversion but simply by collecting, eating and excreting electrons directly. In his research he found eight types of electricity-eating bacteria. In order to study them, he stuck a few electrodes into the soil and set them to different voltages. If bacteria are present, they connect up between the electrodes. The bacteria not only appear to consume electricity, but also to pass it on to each other by forming filaments in the sediment so that the electricity can move around. Although they do not need energy-rich nutrients such as sugars or other organic molecules to grow, they do need trace elements such as phosphorus, sulphur and nitrogen. This entire process is very similar to that of photosynthetic organisms, but with electricity instead of light [19*].

It is one thing for a few microbes to navigate and communicate with the geomagnetic field, but this is something altogether different. A great mystery that had lain hidden in mud pools, riverbeds and at the bottom of the great ocean for centuries on end, began to reveal its secrets now, one after the other. Coherence started to appear in over 40 years of research into geomagnetic life forms that did not have to collect their intelligence themselves, as humans do, but participated directly in the intelligence of the geomagnetic field.

We look up into the sky and do not see the electromagnetic activities of the geomagnetic field. We see an empty sky. We therefore come to the conclusion that we are alone here, separated lives searching and striving for insight, truth, perception. But take a moment to consider a mud pool, for it contains all kinds of bacteria that respond to the inclination, direction and speed of the causative electromagnetic forces of the geomagnetic field present in the mud pool. While we think we do not notice these forces, the geomagnetic intelligence is available all around us and within us. If there is one thing that is clear, it is that the behaviour of bacteria is completely determined by it. For them, concepts of individuality and collectivity seem non-existent. Geomagnetic field alignment seems to be the first principle of bacteria. What is the geomagnetic field like today? What does it want? What can I do for it? What if we asked ourselves those same questions? For bacteria, everything begins in the geomagnetic field; they live in coexistence with it.

 ## Solutions for self-inflicted problems

This fascinating bacterial EM life also has a downside. Our ignorant interference in the EMST dynamics of their existence constitutes a great risk. We are causing something that is potentially irreversible and are inciting a world full of potential friends to turn against us. After all, bacteria and possibly viruses can multiply and change as a result of exposure to EMFs but may also be killed by them. Research into EMST and the specific frequencies to which bacteria and viruses are sensitive, or which they use for their life functions or their ways of communication, is virtually non-existent. This poses enormous dangers. What if the increasingly dense human generated electrosoup, which is spreading like an oil slick across the entire ecosystem, starts killing the good bacteria and multiplying the harmful bacteria? This is not just about the risks we take with the microbes that live far away in a rubbish dump near a slum or at the bottom of an ocean. After all, more than 100,000 billion microbes live on a human body, and each person carries on average 2 kilos of bacteria in body weight. To a large extent, the state of those bacterial colonies on and in our bodies combined is responsible for our personal well-being. The balance between useful bacterial colonies and destructive bacterial colonies determines whether we stay healthy or become ill. What if the increasingly dense electrosoup irreversibly tilts the balance between these colonies? The bacteria sympathize with us, follow our way of life, react to how we think and what we expose ourselves to. 60% of life on earth consists of microorganisms. Humans, animals and plants completely pale into insignificance compared to this. On average, as many bacteria live in our mouths as there are stars in the galaxy, about 100 billion. The number of viruses is even greater. For example, a drop of seawater contains more than one million bacteria, but it contains ten million viruses. Viruses are therefore the most common life forms on earth. And when we start making phone calls, we are not alone; on a mobile phone some 4,000 bacteria per cm^2 are listening in. The bacterial colony lodged on a mobile phone is much larger than the bacterial colony on a toilet seat.

With all the knowledge we are gaining about bacteria since Antoni van Leeuwenhoek first started perceiving them through his self-manufactured microscope, we still form an incorrect image about them. We think of them as isolated life forms. They are not. Most of nature's bacteria occur in close-knit communities that are connected in many ways by electromagnetic signals. They live preferably in biofilms on teeth, hands and feet, sinks, toilet seats and in sewage pipes, on rocks, in bays and oceans. Because the electromagnetic context of these biofilms has not yet penetrated the collective consciousness, there is only some exploratory research available. Although very few lived with the reality of bacteria in the 17th century, many became ill from it, and although very few in the 21st century live with the reality that artificial EMFs might have a decisive impact on the way bacteria and viruses behave, many are probably already experiencing the consequences. Respect is appropriate about the fact that microbes are by far the majority of life forms on earth.

Think of hospitals, for example. Parallel to the advancement of the internet of things, the hospital bacterium, which is still difficult to kill with traditional antibiotics, is also advancing. It is a growing problem in hospitals all over the world. A study from 2016 shows that electromagnetic signals with specific high frequencies and low intensities can trigger antibiotic resistance in bacteria. Without adding things up, EMST may have become a major risk factor in hospitals. Bacteria and cells communicate with each other via electromagnetic signals with a high frequency range. These EMFs influence the *Escherichia coli*, for example. The EMFs inhibit their growth and change their properties. The effects are not thermal. The targets of the effects of EMFs in cells can be water, cell plasma membrane and genetics. The risk of EMFs interaction with bacteria therefore includes among other things the change in their susceptibility to antibiotics [20*]. Conversely, researchers discovered four years earlier that an electric plasma can kill the superbacteria in hospitals. They found the weak spot in the armour of superbacteria such as MRSA. An electrically charged plasma beam seems to drive the resistant colonies apart, making it much easier to kill them [21*]. In this way, we are discovering more and more solutions to problems that we ourselves may be creating. Other examples of the possible impact of artificial EMFs on the natural functioning of bacteria are described in the chapter on the consequences for animals and plants.

Aware but not necessarily intelligent

Caution seems to be required. Perhaps intelligence is not the strongest side of humans. Perhaps our function is much more reflected in the open-minded, curious spontaneity with which

Antoni van Leeuwenhoek looked at the world and the way in which he, for example, cherished lice and lice eggs on his legs and in his socks in order to have enough microbes to observe. When it comes to the intelligence that is embedded in social order, structures and discipline, we can learn from the ants, the bacteria or the elephants. When it comes to the intelligence that lies in elegance, gracefulness and beauty, we can learn from a swarm of starlings or a school of fish, among other things. When it comes to the intelligence that lies in peaceful coexistence and harmony, we can learn, among other things, from a forest full of different trees. When it comes to the intelligence that is embedded in durability and reliability, then we can learn from just about all participants in life on Earth, except from humans. In connection with the electromagnetic fields, bacteria subconsciously and almost carelessly do the most incredibly intelligent things all the time. By trying to unravel the secrets of their intelligence we gather awareness about it: awareness in the sense of appreciation, inspiration, perception, cognition, amazement and many other things. Can we give back to nature that kind of consciousness about the natural intelligence of the ecosystem?

Bacterial circuits

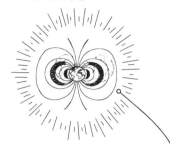

Bacteria share life functions with each other via EMST. Some bacteria can breathe for the entire colony, while others can eat for the entire colony. Conversion to EMFs does the rest

Bacteria, including the good ones, can be altered as well as destroyed by artificial EMFs

Radiation from masts and mobile phones can cause bacterial colonies to proliferate or even cause them to self-destruct. Moulds, for example, seem to multiply massively under EMF influence

Artificial EMFs can make bacteria resistant to antibiotics

Bacteria produce magnets that allow them to fully align to the geomagnetic field

Bacteria form an integrated circuit with the geomagnetic field

Bacteria produce electricity and can store it in their bodies

Some bacteria live in intel-ligent electrically integrated circuits of overwhelming visual beauty

Viruses loaded with specific EMFs can kill bacteria

Bacterial colonies form wired communication networks using nanowires and also maintain wire-less contacts with other colonies. The DNA length seems to determine the frequency of the bacterial telephony

Cells

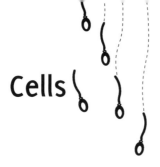

How it is possible that
low-intensity EMFs have
more impact on cells
than high-intensity EMFs

Russian geochemist Vladimir Vernadsky proceeded on the basis that the all-pervasive influence and effect of EMFs from space not only influence the functioning of the geomagnetic sphere, but that these cosmic signals also play a crucial role in the evolution and the behaviour and composition of all life on earth. He considered that all processes on earth could only be understood from the causal influence of intergalactic processes. In his view, all manifestations on earth were a physically anchored electromagnetic reflection of various specific cosmic electromagnetic processes. In his book 'The Biosphere', Vernadsky wrote that living organisms are the fruit of complex cosmic processes and form an essential part of a universally harmonious mechanism that works through laws of nature [1*].

All living organisms are made up of cells and form a cellular ecosystem, and each individual cell has, in principle, all characteristics of life. Is it inconceivable that the largest of all, the galactic sphere and its radiation frequencies, can exert a direct influence on the tiniest of all, i.e. cells and DNA, through a complex system of electromagnetic filters? This chapter deals with the smallest possible and the next chapter with the largest possible.

Robert Hooke, in 1665, was the first to discover the cell. His discoveries included honeycomb structures in cork and other plant material which reminded him of monks' cells, so he called them cells. Based on current knowledge, it seems that a human has approximately 20,000 genes and the honeybee approximately 10,000. The function of 97% of human DNA is still unknown.

This explains why it is, probably mistakenly, called junk DNA. After all, just because we do not know the function of something does not mean it is waste.

The body's ability to heal itself seems to depend partly on the natural electric fields of the body. Cell migration and cell division play a key role in that healing process. The vast majority of researches in this area relate to chemical factors, but different studies have demonstrated that exposing cells to electric fields might have a major impact on cell migration and cell division. Cell division seems in any case to be driven by natural internal electric fields. One of the things scientists are attempting now is to promote the healing of spinal cord injury by generating an electric field, because a positively charged electric field can attract proteins and lipids from cell membranes. Stronger fields also seem to encourage cells to divide, but how this is done is not clear. Researchers claim that natural electric fields in the body play a key role in healing [2*].

But what about electromagnetic signal transference, or EMST, involved in the emergence of life? Is there any possible evidence to support the causal presence of natural EMFs in the emergence of life?

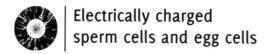 Electrically charged
sperm cells and egg cells

Female *muriqui* monkeys are capable of altering their vaginal electrical potential in such a way that they can direct fertilization by X or Y spermatozoa to maintain the balance between males and females in their group. So they are able to do this by means of electrical signals [3*].

Everything we do with our body is possible because electrical impulses pass through it. Even where life begins, everything seems to revolve around electricity and magnetism, such as the seemingly electrically driven process of fertilization. In that case, the X spermatozoon has a negative charge and the Y spermatozoon builds up a positive charge. This fact was observed when the X and Y spermatozoa were separated by electrophoresis. Specific sperm cells with different sex chromosomes were instantly attracted by the anode (+) or the cathode (-), depending on their distinctive characteristics [4*].

Further studies revealed that when a weak electric current was passed through a solution containing spermatozoa, those with the X chromosome were attracted by the anode and those with the Y chromosome by the cathode. Later, scientists discovered that the ovum membrane has an electric charge, too. Because the ovum's charge can alternate between positive and negative, it will sometimes attract the X- and sometimes the Y-bearing spermatozoon [5*]. This is called the polarity cycle of the membrane. Scientists at the University of Roscoff, France, identified the appearance of a brief luminous ring at the moment of contact between sperm cell and egg cell [6*].

The electric charge of the ovum membrane is not fixed but is estimated to be 60 millivolts on average. The membrane around a human egg cell emits ions and transfers a type of electric charge from itself. In addition, the researchers noticed a distinct electromagnetic neutral period in the cycle when the electric charge surrounding an egg completely depends on environmental factors. When the time of the fertile period has arrived, the egg always carries a negative charge and the spermatozoon a positive one. Because of the fact that opposite charges attract one another, the negatively charged egg attracts those millions of positively charged spermatozoa towards itself. They are all drawn in, but with the first sperm cell that is able to penetrate the egg, the electric charge changes instantly. It seems that once that particular spermatozoon has found access the egg changes its electric field, making it impenetrable to other sperm cells by using EMST [7*].

A resulting hypothesis is that the electric charge of all other sperm cells transfers via EMST to the one that made it. This conjecture is supported by the existence of the superconductive ecology around the egg at the moment of fertilization. Consequently, there is no environment of competition at the point of fertilization, but an environment of mutual support in which the success of that one sperm means the success of all spermatozoa. In this hypothesis, the electrical essences of all 60 to 300 million spermatozoa will be passed on via EMST to that one spermatozoid that has gained access. Their electrical life energy is an integral part of the emergence of new life. None of the charge is lost and competition is non-existent.

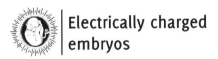 ## Electrically charged embryos

Vladimir Vernadsky basically regarded each individual organism as an extension of, and inseparably bound up with, the whole geomagnetic sphere. Because he believed that the causality of the larger cosmic context continued in the much smaller planetary ecosystem, he looked for a new understanding of all organisms on earth as uniquely organized electromagnetic processes. Vernadsky's ideas experienced a revival in the work of Colin Lowry, 'The Electrical Embryo', in which he substantiates the way electric fields shape embryonic growth patterns. As an example, experiments are discussed in which aspects of the electromagnetic fields of salamander embryos are manipulated in such a way that significant changes occur in the whole embryo [8*].

This means that the function of the electric field is not just limited to organising local cell migrations, but that the influence extends over and over again to the organisation of all embryonic growth patterns. The fact that the fate of a single cell is always linked to developments in the entire organism had been known for a very long time, but the theories and findings of Vernadsky, Lowry and others revealed the mechanism of that electromagnetic bond of common fate. This discovery shows that cells from their first division are entangled with the field of the whole. The division is the confirmation of coherence. This was also the way in which Vernadsky looked at the influence of cosmic EMFs on all electromagnetic processes on earth.

What methods may be available to cells to determine their position in the whole of the growing embryo? What is decisive for cell differentiation? Firstly, cells appear capable of receiving, detecting and emitting EMFs also in the far infrared range. Cells have a type of visual faculty that enables them to respond to those electromagnetic signals [9*]. Secondly, electromagnetic radiation in the further ultraviolet range appears capable of organising cell division. With this, we seem to become aware of an increasingly differentiated electromagnetic communication mechanism that directs embryonic growth and development using

EMST from the earliest stage of an organism's life [10*, 11*]. The question arises: in what ways do cells make even further use of the language and frequencies of the electromagnetic spectrum to communicate with their immediate surroundings and possibly a larger context?

Vernadsky would have been delighted with this substantial body of evidence, because cells not only have methods at their disposal to determine their position in the whole of the growing embryo, but also have, potentially, the ability to align to the higher spheres of the earth's magnetic field.

 ## Cells with fractal antennae and outer planetary connections

Human cells have electric fields as powerful as lightning. Researchers found this by using newly developed voltage sensitive nanoparticles which they tested in brain tumour fluid. Electric fields of 15 million volts per metre were identified. Even though the existence of electric fields around cell membranes is a well-known phenomenon in cell biology, this discovery goes far beyond that [12*]. It can change the whole way we look at the origins of disease.

As early as 1985, a researcher concluded that microwaves can cause changes in nerve cells. The results showed that the spontaneous activity of snails is restrained when snail neurons are subjected to electromagnetic radiation with a 2.45 GHz frequency [13*]. In 2003, mammalian brain nerve cells were found to be damaged by exposure to microwaves from mobile phones [14*]. Then, in 2011, research was carried out to see whether DNA acts as a fractal antenna in electromagnetic fields. The results demonstrated that EMF interactions with DNA gave the same results over a wide range of frequencies, and the conclusion was drawn that DNA does indeed work as a fractal antenna. This means greater DNA reactivity to EMFs, and DNA damage may be an explanation for the increase in cancer epidemics [15*]. Another study demonstrated that exposure to EMFs in the GHz range can (1) change transport through cellular membranes, (2) alter the activity in cell membranes, (3) interfere with DNA, (4) influence the cell cycle and (5) cause genetic instability [16*].

In addition to the risk to which DNA in cells is exposed due to the antenna function of increasing artificial EMFs in the present times, there is also the proposition of a third method which potentially enables cells to tune to the larger context. The first two methods are: (1) visual ability of cells to see EMFs in the infrared range, and (2) radiation from the ultraviolet range that appears capable of organising cell division. The third method is: (3) the antenna function of cell DNA which basically enables them to communicate with various natural planetary and outer planetary sources of these frequencies within the GHz range.

Immortal cells by unlimited electromagnetic tissue regeneration

Contrary to most multicellular animals, flatworms regenerate all their body parts after the parts are removed. They have the unbelievable ability to infinitely regenerate tissue. In all instances, electromagnetic activity appears to be the first step in the process of tissue regeneration, even before any genetic machinery is set in motion to construct new heads and tails. It is important to understand how cells decide on what to build. The internal electrical signals generated by flatworm cells provide the ability to reconstruct organs by means of internal EMST. When parts of these flatworms are removed, the remaining tissue regenerates the missing bits at the correct end, whether a head or a tail.

Previous studies have shown that about six hours after amputation, the first genes associated with regenerating a missing part are electrically activated. Until now, it was not known what mechanisms control which genes are turned on. The researchers used voltage-sensitive fluorescent dyes which made it possible to literally see the electric activity in the tissue. How do regenerated tissues decide on the size and shape of the body parts they reconstruct and how do bioelectric circuits store changes in body patterns? Charged ions constantly pass in and out of cells, giving cells a natural electric charge. The patterns of electrical activity are thought to play an important role in controlling how embryos develop limbs. A flatworm with a particular gene expression and stem cell distribution does not store its body's blueprint in tissue or stem cells, but in electrical frequencies and signals [17*]. This is remarkable, because this means that genetic change takes place by means of electrical signals.

Observing electrical causal mechanisms in mammals is the next step. The human body is able to regenerate an accidentally cut-off piece of finger. Do electrical signals also direct regeneration in humans? That would constitute a paradigm shift. The perception about the electromagnetic ecosystem is spreading in all directions. Researchers hope their discoveries will be useful for the health of humans and animals. Could electrical signals become a replacement for medication? Are some forms of cancer in animals and humans possibly attempts by the body to decipher the artificial radiation codes as if they were causing evolution? Did people subconsciously use nature's electromagnetic language by exploiting it through artificial wireless techniques? What do these new radiation techniques then do with, for example, the electromagnetic process of tissue regeneration in flatworms?

Cells prefer silent energy signals

While some consider all living things as physical bags of chemicals, it is now much more accurate, based on state-of-the-art cell biology, to consider the essence of all life as a dynamic energetic signature. It seems that life can be much better understood in terms of energy frequencies. The energy frequencies that organise a bee colony are possibly entangled as well as continuously interacting with the energy frequencies of other bee colonies, plants and animals. The above shows that even more exciting and deeper layers of hardly-researched contextual electromagnetic communication take place at the level of cells in animals and plants. Humans also communicate instinctively with the same electromagnetic signals at all these levels. All organisms are therefore designed to be able to communicate and make connections with the entire electrical web of life that extends far beyond the boundaries of the geomagnetic sphere. Hardly any fish, bird, insect or bacteria species exist that do not participate in the continuous interaction with that much bigger context. The central organising principle in nature, as we understand it now, seems to focus increasingly on reading electrical frequencies.

When a cell is given two kinds of information, i.e. chemical information and electrical information, electrical signals will always be 100 times more efficient in regulating cell functions than chemical ones. Would EMFs be able to replace drugs in due course? This calls for a re-evaluation of the entire ecosystem. We ought to reconsider the ecosystem in the context of electromagnetic signalling, otherwise we cannot understand millions of ways in which the cells in our body, the cells in insects, bacteria, cows and chickens communicate with each other and with the earth's magnetic field through electric signalling and frequencies. Without ever being aware of it before, we are living in an intelligent electromagnetic ecosystem that works by using its own internet of things. According to Bruce Lipton, it is especially the 'silent energy' in this energetic ecosystem that influences biology most [18].

The difficulty with radiation in the GHz range is that it works with the same frequency and energy intensities that cells use to intercommunicate. New transmissions in the GHz range will operate with weak or silent energy intensities. This is why transmission masts will be positioned close to each other (300 metres) and also close to homes, offices and across nature reserves to ensure that self-driving cars, for instance, can indeed drive independently. This seems a major advantage, because weak signals would be less harmful than strong signals. Naturally, such strong signals will inevitably cause heat damage in the GHz range. But researchers anticipate that weak or silent signals in the GHz range will definitely have a direct effect on communication among cells and the cells in conjunction with the larger context. This cell-confusing or cell-manipulating risk is not common knowledge yet, has hardly been studied and is not recognised yet, partly because it involves uncomfortable dilemmas and partly because the scientific discoveries underpinning these risks are quite recent [19, 20].

Cells operate at identical frequencies to the ones that will be used by the latest wireless technologies, i.e. weak or silent signals. To understand the biological effects of weak EMFs, it is important to see that the strongest signals are not always the most harmful ones. The view is still held that, if cells are affected by electrical signals, the rule should apply that when the signal is stronger, the effect is greater. But this is not true. The idea that weaker electromagnetic signals have little to no biological effects is no longer valid and is based on the assumption that only the thermal risks of EMFs on biological tissue should be avoided. Turning the signal volume control low would suffice in that case. However, the effect of electrical signals on biological materials would require thorough investigation by mapping out how and to what extent those signals would confuse human, animal and plant cells in a non-thermal way. Weak EMFs can be very bio-informative and cause serious biological effects. As an example, a collective research project has been carried out into the biological effects of 2.45 GHz EMFs on brain cells, fertility, cell cycle, cell membranes, memory and behaviour in general [21*].

How mobile phones
can ring cells

Nerve cells, for example, communicate with each other in extremely weak potentials. Things that generate weak signals, such as mobile phones and the dirty electricity dancing on the electromagnetic fields around live wires in walls, may certainly have an effect on body cells [22*, 23*]. They regard them as instructions because the information is supplied to them in the same form as the geomagnetic field does. But the artificially generated silent signals carry no food or messages for the cells. They are empty, and possibly cause cellular level disease. Furthermore, the weak but natural impulses the geospheric field transfers to our cells have all kinds of powerful effects on the biological material. As will be explored in the following chapter, Higher Spheres, cells are also impacted by natural heliospheric influences, among other things.

In principle, any electric field can transfer information by means of impulse and frequency fluctuations. This means that mobile phones could also instruct our body cells when we are having a phone call. Healthy biological organisms have coherent electromagnetic fields and unhealthy organisms have electromagnetic fields that work with disturbed and fragmented signals.

By activating new wireless systems that probably become increasingly operational in the higher GHz range, all kinds of symptoms can be expected that have never occurred before in humans, animals and plants. The cells can, in fact, receive these frequencies and impulses as new instructions. With our human choices we hold the future of the entire ecosystem in the palm of our hand.

Cell Phone

The body encourages its healing process by internal electric fields

Electrical signals are 100 times more efficient in regulating cell activities than chemicals

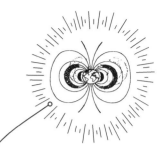

Cells can tune to the larger context of the geomagnetic field, because the cell's DNA can act as an antenna

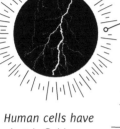

Human cells have electric fields as powerful as lightning. Researchers identified electric fields of 15 million volts per metre

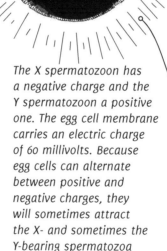

Electric fields determine embryonic growth patterns

Cell division is directed by electric fields

The X spermatozoon has a negative charge and the Y spermatozoon a positive one. The egg cell membrane carries an electric charge of 60 millivolts. Because egg cells can alternate between positive and negative charges, they will sometimes attract the X- and sometimes the Y-bearing spermatozoa

2.45 GHz EMFs affect cell neurons of snails and restrain their activities

Higher Spheres

How the different electromagnetic spheres influence each other and remain strictly separated in levels at the same time

How far does the electric ecosystem extend? Based on what has already been stated, we know that the brains and bodies of many animals contain crystal formations, strings of neurons or other techniques capable of dealing with magnetic information. We know that bacteria, bees, cells, fruit flies, pigeons and turtles can tune to the geospheric internet of things in various ways.

In addition, there is good reason to assume that all kinds of entanglements occur where it is not, say, bacteria themselves that tune into the geosphere, but where an entire colony of bacteria acts as a connected geosphere extension. It means that when we observe, using microscopes, the behaviour of bacterial colony, we are in fact observing the behaviour of the geomagnetic field. Based on that view, the beauty of the patterns that can form in a biofilm is a product of geomagnetic intelligence and not bacterial intelligence.

A number of important questions will be addressed in this chapter: to what extent can the earth's magnetic field, or the geosphere, tune into other higher spheres? To what extent does the interaction between various higher spheres also work by means of electricity and magnetism? And, if the mother of the intelligent beauty of a colony of bacteria, a school of fish or a flight of birds is the geosphere itself, how does the entanglement function on other levels? Are there indications for electromagnetic entanglement between planets, their moons and the heliosphere? How far does the electric ecosystem extend?

If a reasonable case can be made that the electric ecosystem does in fact extend far beyond the geosphere, this raises other questions, such as: is there a connection between the natural EMFs of planetary origin and the moon? After all, the moon is an inert rock. Or is it? And there are further questions such as: are there any electromagnetic signal exchanges between the geosphere and the heliosphere or between the geosphere and the galactosphere? How does heliospheric, or even galactospheric entanglement actually work? Is it conceivable that humans or animals suffer from symptoms prompted by heliospheric EMFs? Is it conceivable that galactospheric or heliospheric EMFs cause changes in behaviour, temper, mood, health or even genetic material, as suggested by Carl Sagan in 1973? In a film clip that is still available on YouTube, he speaks about the way cosmic radiations cause gradual mutations in human, animal and also plant DNA. In what way is the interconnectedness of the higher spheres, galactosphere and heliosphere expressed in daily life in the geosphere? Are all these spheric levels interwoven into an integrated electric ecosystem by means of EMFs? At this point, we exchange the microscope for the telescope.

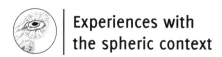 ## Experiences with the spheric context

Probably everyone has experienced a moment of intimate connection with the greater universal context in which we live, for example, when as a child we stood outside at night, coming face to face with the immensity of the starry sky. There can be a feeling of one's own insignificance and the deep-felt desire to give expression to it whilst we are standing there, alone, but connected to the huge world above us. These are special moments with something that is not easy to comprehend, but which we all know is very close to us. A night under the stars in Cornwall causes the same deep and nearly indescribable feelings of entanglement with the universe as a night under the stars in Tennessee, Nairobi or Jerusalem. The impact, intimacy and indescribable feelings of cohesion and connectedness are exactly the same and can wordlessly be shared with anyone. At that moment, while our eyes search the immeasurable skies in vain for a boundary, a definition, a shape or a recognisable order, our small self down here is lovingly transported up to where it becomes part of the vast ocean of dotted lights. So far away and yet... so close. So incomprehensibly vast and yet... so completely visible as the tiny little hairs on an arm.

For one moment it is possible, anywhere in the world, to feel how our own microcosm is an integral part of the macrocosm. Some people have been able to describe these experiences, those moments where the universe swallowed them, by depicting the macrocosm as a mirror in which they saw their human condition accurately reflected. Others have spoken of an experience which told them they had been created in the image of the universe. Even though the feeling of 'as above, so below' is very real and potent in those moments, there is still more.

For the children of North African nomads those moments, when the starry sky briefly swallows them, are not different from the experiences of farmers' children in Central Australia. The message that there is no fundamental difference in the order to which a human belongs and the order from which the Milky Way originated, reaches us always and everywhere. The small is reflected in the large, in the same way that a tiny little cell in the human body is genetically reflected in the possibilities of the whole human system.

Now, with the most modern methods, it is possible to bring that sense of wonder and the resulting connection to a next level of spheric insights.

Birth of
the moon

Planets such as Mercury, the Earth and Jupiter, which each have their own magnetic field, are protected by the spheres of influence they generate. Jupiter's electromagnetic sphere of influence is so extensive that its moons, Io, Europe, Ganymede and Callisto, can 'swim' in it permanently. They are still in an embryonic state there, as it were [1*].

That is partly the case for our moon. Every month it gets an energy boost during its seven day stay inside the tail of the geomagnetic field. The moon is moving around freely in the electric field of the heliosphere under the influence of the sun for the remainder of the month. Thus, the moon is alternately fed under the influence of the electromagnetic impulses and frequencies from the sun and the earth.

The earth's magnetic field has a head and tail and looks like a fish. That tail is huge and stretches far beyond the orbit of the moon, with a length of approximately 46 earth diameters or 600,000 kilometres. The head, which is always pointed towards the sun, has a size of about 5 earth diameters or 65,000 kilometres. For 7 days every month, the moon inevitably hides behind the earth's nocturnal side, bathing in the electromagnetic geospheric influences.

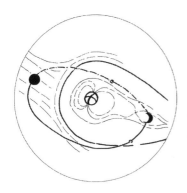

The moon completes one rotation in about 28 days, being under the influence of the sun for 21 days and under the influence of the earth for 7 days

Whenever the moon is full, it is inside the tail of the geomagnetic field, or magneto-tail, and strange things happen on the lunar surface. Fine dust particles can suddenly rise up from the ground. This is because they are being charged by the electrical influences of the magneto-tail. During its crossing of the tail, the moon comes into contact with the super charged plasma of hot particles that are active in the magneto-tail. These particles give the moon a negative charge. Astronauts avoid the moon like the plague when this happens.

The *Lunar Prospector,* the NASA spacecraft that circled the moon many times when it travelled through the magneto-tail, registered huge electric changes on the surface of the moon with power surges up to 1,000 volts. The electrically charged plasma zones of the geosphere have a dynamic structure. They are in constant motion. One moment the moon may swim around in a perfectly calm plasma sea, while the next moment it suddenly ends up in a turbulent zone of the magneto-tail that electrifies the entire lunar surface. Intensity of electrical impulses reaches a peak during the solar and geospheric storms. As stated, the magneto-tail of the geosphere is not the only source of electrical energy charging the moon. The solar winds essentially feed the moon with many more charged particles, but as soon as the moon whizzes into the magneto-tail, the solar wind influence is reduced to an absolute minimum and the moon falls entirely under the geospheric influence. The geosphere plasma zone is generally ten times hotter than the solar wind. After the moon has entered the geosphere, seven intensive geosphere feeding days begin. This is the way in which the sun and the earth feed the moon in turn with different frequencies [2,3].

There are all kinds of theories about the birth of the moon. The fact is that the composition of the moon is very similar to that of the earth. Nevertheless, there is a theory stating that the moon was formed elsewhere in the solar system and was then captured in the earth's gravity. Then there is the theory stating that the moon and the earth were jointly condensed from interstellar gas clouds of charged particles, from which the whole solar system was formed too. According to that theory, the solar system therefore originated from the same nebula. But the most popular and most accepted theory is that a planet the size of Mars accidentally collided with the earth, just after the formation of the solar system. Enormous amounts of heated material from the outer layers of both celestial bodies escaped from that collision. This material then clumped together to form the moon. In this, the moon is the result of a coincidental confrontation.

But what if there is an alternative for this genesis? What if the moon was not created by a frontal collision, but by a natural process of birth? What if the moon in essence was born from the earth? In 2007, a petrologist and geophysicist found new evidence for the idea that the moon was born from the earth. This would also help to explain why the moon distances itself 4 centimetres from the earth each year. In this thinking, the more the moon matures, the more it will feel the natural urge to claim its own place in space [4].

So, the genesis of the moon is still unknown. Of all the possible theories about this, this book holds the view on the moon being one of the young, growing offspring of the large family of celestial bodies. That image best fits this chronicle which proposes that everything in the electric ecosystem is interconnected.

The lunar sphere: the development of a lunar magnetic field

If it is true that the moon was born from the earth and started a process of maturing under the maternal influence of the earth, what then are the indications for the development of a so-called lunar magnetic field? After all, without a lunar magnetic field the moon is incapable of dealing selectively with the immense flow of electrically charged particles flying through space. And without such a selective electromagnetic field no atmosphere can be created.

In 2010, first mention was made of a small part of the lunar surface that could shield itself from the solar wind. This appearance of a mini magnetosphere was observed close to the lunar equator, where sunlight can only penetrate half of the time. There are indications for more small magnetospheres on the moon. India's Chandrayaan-1 lunar probe confirmed the development of miniature versions of a magnetosphere by the moon that protect small parts of the lunar surface in the northeast section of the dark side of the moon. It is that part of the moon that averts its face from the earth. So far, the largest magnetosphere observed on the moon has a diameter of approximately 360 kilometres [5*].

Because the moon has not yet developed a full lunar magnetic field, the electromagnetically charged particles from the sun, from the earth and from cosmic radiation are still raining down freely on the moon's surface. There are indications that the moon is developing its own electromagnetic sphere. The moon is charged by the heliospheric solar wind and the geomagnetic field. So you could say that both frequencies together provide some kind of father and mother influence on the young moon. In this way, the sun and the earth jointly form a fertile electric ecosystem for the moon.

The sun currently has the most dominant influence on the moon for about 21 days a month, when the moon goes outside the magneto-tail of the earth, swimming in the flow of the heliosphere. During the 7-day period of the month when the moon is inside the tail of the geosphere, the moon falls under the earth's maternal supervision – it takes on its electromagnetic education. How does that work?

Whenever the moon enters the earth's geosphere, the lunar sphere grows

According to the latest observations, the moon, whenever it is inside the geosphere tail, is developing a very powerful electric field. Charged particles from the magnetic tail of the geosphere are then absorbed by the lunar surface, especially when the moon travels through the core of the magneto-tail where the charges increase tremendously. It is as if the moon is in brief contact with the electric umbilical cord of the earth. The dayside of the moon then becomes positively charged by solar radiation that liberates electrons from the lunar surface, while the electrons on the nightside of the moon are actually building up and give the lunar surface a negative charge. This way, the lunar sphere seems to be slowly developing a dipole field for itself in the image of the earth's geosphere [6*]. The moon is charging itself as a giant battery.

To crown it all, the SELENE, a Japanese spacecraft, discovered in 2017 that the moon 'breathes' – the moon collects oxygen from the earth. It gets a huge daily dose of high-energy solar radiation. But in the 7 days inside the magneto-tail, it appears that oxygen from different plants on earth rises and ends up on the moon in enormous quantities. So, it rains oxygen on the moon throughout these 7 days. Probes from the SELENE spacecraft detected charged oxygen atoms minus one electron on the lunar surface. This high-energy oxygen was not detected when the moon was outside the magneto-tail [7*]. The moon breathes in deeply each time it travels through the tail, as it were.

 ## The geosphere: the development of a spheric frame of reference

As the years of the 20th and 21st century passed by, the starry sky was further probed by new instruments. And a new stunning frame of reference was given to something that everybody knew in their hearts already by simply looking up: the spheric universe. It started not long ago with the discovery of the earth's magnetic field, a field that not only consists of radiation, but a field that has layers and levels in which specific force fields prevail. These Van Allen radiation belts, as they are called, give the earth an enormous sphere of influence that extends far into space [8*].

Without this ordered energy field, all life on earth would

disappear very rapidly because of the powerful waves from the sun's radiation and the interstellar winds. This reveals the first purpose of the geosphere: protecting life on earth. For some, this is the beginning and the end. Case closed. The planetary sphere simply exists. This is it. And then there are those who are still looking up full of wonder, for instance at the interplay of forces of the Northern Lights, as a reflection of the way the geosphere protects the earth against solar winds. They not only see the protective effect of the geosphere, but also the magnificent colours appearing due to contact between the heliospheric and geospheric influences. They may ask themselves the question: if the earth has a geosphere that interacts with the heliosphere of the sun, does it follow that we have a biosphere that interacts with these spheres? Could our biosphere have been created in the image of the magnetic field of the earth? And what if our biosphere interacts with the geosphere? Would we perhaps also be able to see the electromagnetic colours of the Northern Lights in our own sphere? And this is just the beginning of the development of a spheric frame of reference.

The geomagnetic sphere of the earth is the first sphere outside our biosphere or sphere of influence. It stretches far above the planetary surface to a location in space where it meets the solar wind and forms a shield against the flow of electromagnetic particles that are fired from the sun to the earth every single second. Measured on the earth's surface, the magnetic force of the geosphere varies from 25 to 65 microtesla. The field appears to currently manifest as a dipole, but at the same time contains multipole functionalities that seem to be becoming increasingly strong now.

Research shows that the connection between geospheric fields and plant reactions is much more important than previously assumed. Plants have the ability to react quickly to varying magnetic fields by changing themselves genetically. Furthermore, as mentioned earlier, there are bacteria that have the ability as a complete colony to orient themselves on the geomagnetic field. A 2014 study expressed concerns about the impact of artificial EMFs on the functioning of magnetite crystals in the natural communication between animals and plants and the geosphere [9*].

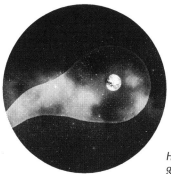

Humans, animals and plants live IN the geosphere rather than ON the earth

The geosphere protects all life against a radiation overdose from the universe, but it also lets through radiations from the electromagnetic spectrum that are necessary for life and evolution. As an example, the geosphere has created an optic window in the electromagnetic spectrum so that all those spectral frequencies – which we know as light – can pass. Without light, there is no life. But other specific frequencies are also allowed on earth. Life on earth has evolved under the influence of changes in the power and composition of the geosphere. The original evolution of bacteria, for example, seems to have been inspired by the lightning and the powerful electromagnetic charges associated with it. Because electric shocks are used in laboratories to genetically manipulate bacteria, researchers suggested that lightning could have the same gene-changing effect. To substantiate their theory, they exposed bacteria to electric shocks from artificially generated lightning. Two strains of the *Pseudomonas* soil bacterium and the *E. coli* bacterium showed the expected results. Bacteria were genetically altered using the artificial lightning bolt [10*]. It has also become known that lightning itself is triggered by interactions between the geosphere and solar winds. The way bacteria and higher life forms evolve may well have its origin in the natural EMFs that develop from the interaction between the geomagnetic field and higher spheres. The selective windows created by the geomagnetic field seem to inspire changes in the organisation of life.

Artificial EMFs are not designed to cause evolution, however. They serve an economic purpose, not an evolutionary one. They are radiation fields which are transmitted along with various random messages. Nobody knows what these messages cause in humans, animals and plants. It is also unknown what the influence will be of the interaction between artificial GHz transmissions from the latest satellites and the naturally generated background radiations of the geosphere. What will be the fate of the beach fleas orienting on the geomagnetic field [11*] now that so many artificial electromagnetic fields are being produced? What do mealworm beetles feel as a result of countless artificial exposures to magnetic fields that accelerate their process of metamorphosis considerably [12*]? What are the experiences of all kinds of other animals faced with disturbances in their ability to maintain contact with the geosphere? Does it feel like a computer virus to the animals that hacks the software they use to maintain contact with the geosphere? Also, plant growth, metabolism and development appear to be hindered by artificial electromagnetic radiation [13*], which may also interfere with the natural connection of plants with the geosphere and/or the natural background radiation from the earth.

It is still fairly unknown territory, but what then are the

far-reaching ecological consequences of these types of electro-magnetic disturbances of the geospheric connections to animals and plants? The chapter on the consequences for the earth contains more information on the question of whether global coverage by artificial EMFs also means global disconnection for the ecosystem. That chapter deals with the consequences of artificial disturbance of planetary background frequencies.

 ## More ways in which the geosphere is entangled with animals

Approximately 20% of the pineal gland cells of rodents and pigeons respond to changes in both direction and intensity of a magnetic field. Evidence was also found for the involvement of the pineal gland and the central nervous system in the perception and transference of geospheric information [14*]. And humans, like bacteria, land animals, fish and birds, are also capable of navigating the earth's magnetic field, as will be opend up in more detail in the chapter on humans.

The worst tsunami ever recorded in recent human history took place in Sri Lanka on 5 January 2005. It took the lives of thousands of people. The huge tidal waves penetrated inland for kilometres and destroyed people, buildings, trees and roads. The tsunami caused death and destruction, but... not among animals. According to H.D. Ratnayke of the National Wildlife Department in Sri Lanka, no animals were found among the wreckage, the corpses and the debris. No buffaloes or elephants, no rats or rabbits. In the tsunami at Ao Sane beach, near Phuket in Thailand, dogs ran up to the hill tops. And in the Cuddalore District in Tamil Nadu, India, buffaloes, goats and dogs escaped from the beach, as did a nesting colony of flamingos that flew to higher ground. How did the animals know what was going to happen? During excavations at the Roman city of Pompeii, which was buried under a layer of debris caused by eruption of the Vesuvius volcano 1,500 years ago, people were found, frozen in flight and with shock visibly crystallized in their postures forever. But no animals, not a hare or rabbit, mouse or rat. All animals had been informed in advance. What was found under the Vesuvian lava was some livestock that had not been able to escape because it was confined in sheds or behind fences. Also in 1960 in Morocco, when an earthquake killed 15,000 people, it became apparent that a huge area was emptied of animals. Another example of the strange prescience of such events in fauna is that during the severe storms of 1972, 1973, 1976 and 1990, employees of the Dutch State Forestry Service observed how animals in large numbers fled the forests just before storms arrived and millions of trees came crashing down.

There was a lady from Kent who had on average twelve epileptic seizures every week and was completely housebound by her illness, until she got a dog. Nearly one hour before she had a seizure, the dog was able to sense what was about to happen and gently tapped her with his paw so she could get to safety. And when the dog knew she was about to have a seizure while she was having a bath, he would pull the plug [15*].

 ## The heliosphere: the sun is an electric form of life with a tail

In its electric heliospheric shape, the sun has a tail and resembles a giant sperm whale swimming through the plasma waters of the galactosphere. Those electrically charged waters turn out to have a much greater effect on the sun than previously thought.

In some of the most recent theories about the sun, the idea

of an electric sun is beginning to emerge. A sun that does not produce all its energy in the first place through an internal process of nuclear fusion, but that receives an enormous amount of electric energy from the galactic context in which it is located. It is, indeed, not only in the centre of the solar system, but also in an astronomical plasma cloud that allows the sun to receive electrical charges via the Milky Way arm to which it belongs [16*].

The electric solar activity in its turn also has an impact on such things as the navigation capabilities of sperm whales. In the last decades of the previous century, more and more sperm whales became stranded on the beaches along the North Sea. Researchers compared all data from sperm whales stranded in the period from 1712 to 2003 with the data on solar activity during the same period. They discovered that 90% of the cases when sperm whales lost their way and ended up on a beach took place when the sunspot period was levelling off. It can be concluded that there is a link between variations in the earth's magnetic field due to changing energy flows from the sun, and the disorientation that occurs in migrating animals [17*].

Heliosphere with tail swimming in an electric plasma flow

The sun therefore seems to be part of an energy-producing plasma, an immense electrical circuit, to which it makes its contribution. This proposes that we do not live in an empty universe in which suns and stars produce their own energy for their separate piece of space. In the electric universe everything is connected in similar ways and, for example, in the same way as we have seen with the bacterial circuits.

Humans, animals and plants not only respond to the geosphere but also to heliospheric influences. The heliosphere of the sun is the second contextual sphere outside our personal sphere of influence. Aside from the geosphere and heliosphere, humans seem to also use their own biosphere mainly as a filter for what we see and experience. Our individual sphere possibly defines our unique humaneness. It seems to allow us to make choices and create consciousness. Bees, bacteria and frogs are unable to do this. They seem to be inextricably entangled with the geosphere. In 2012, Dieter Broers compiled numerous indications about the inevitable fact and the way heliospheric signals influence our entire life: our thoughts, feelings, dreams and mental make-up [18*].

Animals do not have the ability to form their own ideas, views and principles. They download the blueprint of their character and remain true to it. German researchers who studied satellite photos of thousands of cows worldwide, discovered that cows tuned their bodies again and again towards the earth's magnetic field [19*]. A few years later it became clear that dogs, just like cows, prefer to defecate by tuning to the geomagnetic field. Czech researchers observed 70 dogs for a period of 2 years and discovered that they prefer to defecate by aligning their bodies to the north-south axis of the earth's magnetic field, especially in calm geomagnetic field conditions [20*]. When the sun becomes active, the dogs change direction.

The sun has a similar sphere of influence as the earth. But the dimensions of the heliosphere are immeasurably vaster than those of the geosphere. Over the last few years, NASA has succeeded in making sketches of the shape the heliosphere probably takes in interstellar space, based on measurements made by Voyager 1 and 2 along the heliosphere's boundaries. It is hard to imagine, but the sun's heliosphere encompasses the entire solar system, far beyond Pluto. The dimensions of the heliosphere are millions of times larger than the geosphere but the shape and function of the sphere shows great similarity with the geosphere. We live inside a large planetary sphere that rotates within an even larger sphere itself. This introduces us to our Russian doll reality.

The heliosphere is a vast three-dimensional zone around the sun that not only resembles the shape of the earth's magnetic field, but also its function: filtration, protection, regulation. The electromagnetic plasma generated by the sun creates and maintains the heliosphere. The plasma flow pushes the interstellar winds back that attempt to flood the solar system. Supercharged gases form into clusters and clouds, held together by energy-rich plasma filaments. The heliosphere tames the harsh world of pure galactic electromagnetic potency that fills the Milky Way. The geosphere tames those energies even further, so that they can safely penetrate into the geosphere in derived forms where they exert their subtle influence on our human state. A study into hospital data of 6,000 pregnant women covering a period from 1995 to 2003 revealed that 15% of the foetal heart rate had disturbances that coincided precisely with periods of high geomagnetic activity under the influence of solar winds [21*].

Although the content of the entire heliosphere is dominated by the frequencies and energies produced by the sun, there are also cosmic radiations that break through the filters and protective layers of the heliosphere and colour the heliospheric influence with whatever is happening in the galactosphere at that time. The same thing happens at the level of the geosphere. The content of the entire earth's magnetic field is primarily domina-ted by the frequencies and energies produced by the earth, but there are also energies from the level of the heliosphere and ga-lactosphere that break through the various protective layers of the geosphere to colour the geospheric influence with whatever is happening elsewhere in the universe at that time. So, even though the spheres aim to protect and filter, further evolution inside the spheres seems in fact dependent on the energies and frequencies breaking through the protective layers of the spheres. It is not without risk for ourselves to remain unaware of that context.

Research was done into the connection between geomagne-tic storms, caused by powerful solar activities and, for instance, the occurrence of depression. Observations have shown an in-crease of 36.2% in hospitalizations with the diagnosis of depres-sion during powerful solar activities and geomagnetic storms. It is suspected that this link between intense solar activities, geomagnetic storms and the human finds its origin in the pineal gland [22*].

The geosphere inside the heliosphere

A fascinating compilation study evaluated various types of geo-spheric and heliospheric influences on human health. One of the conclusions drawn from this research was that adverse health effects occur both at very low geomagnetic field intensities and at extremely high geospheric activities due to the impact of the solar wind [23*].

Night-time experiences under the stars in France or on the beaches of Florida deepen the realisation that we sense and experience the energy of those stars under the protective and filtering influence of the higher spheres. When we look at the stars with that indescribable feeling of connection to the universe and the Milky Way, we do not see the filtering layers, but they are there. The impact increases as we become more aware of the fact that we, in essence, travel on board living electromagnetic organisms that rotate inside each other and swim around each other. In doing so, they have made themselves invisible in such a way that we can discover the glory of the enormity of the entire context ourselves without it imposing itself on us. Every human being and every living creature has its very own VIP spot, always and anywhere, which allows a direct view of the stars, right through the earth's and solar spheres. The opportunities of children in a refugee camp in Northern Africa are in this respect identical to the opportunities of children who attend an expensive boarding school in London. The higher perspective that surrounds us all, everywhere and at all times, seems to be the great leveller. The more we look up, the more we feel we are the children of that tremendous perspective.

The galactosphere: the Milky Way is an electric life form with a tail

The larger, spiral, galactospheric life forms that fill the universe are reflected in tiny spiral embryos from which every human has been created. The minuteness and intimacy are potentially exactly the same for everyone anywhere on earth.

The voyage of discovery continued, for very recently it was found that the Milky Way is also shrouded in its own sphere. In September 2012, NASA issued its first animated impression of the galactosphere. According to many calculations, the galactic sphere of influence has a radius of no less than 300,000 light years. Based on data from the Chandra X-Ray observatory, NASA calculated that the mass of this charged sphere, leaving aside the physical mass of stars rotating inside it, can be compared to the mass of all stars in the Milky Way combined. According to NASA, the galactosphere mass more or less equals the total physical mass of all stars. The mystery here is that other giant electromagnetic plasma spheres also seem to have formed up inside the core of the Milky Way. A plasma sphere has formed both above and below the black hole in the centre of the galactosphere. Researchers of the Harvard-Smithsonian Center for Astrophysics discovered these immense egg-shaped energy fields each with a diameter of 25,000 light years. The source of energy from which these electromagnetic plasma spheres have formed up is a huge mystery [24*].

While we watch the immeasurable beauty of stars directly, questions start to come up, such as: what is the galactosphere protecting us from? Is its function identical to that of the other spheres enveloping us? What are the parallels between the geosphere, the heliosphere and the galactosphere? What kind of energies from the intergalactic river of cosmic radiation does this third sphere of influence filter? Can the plasma filaments observed between the various galactospheres be viewed as the data cables of some kind of intergalactic internet of things? Do galactospheres communicate in the same way as bacterial colonies?

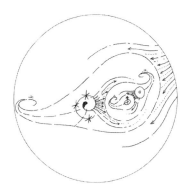

*The galactosphere is
a Russian doll reality*

Here, too, at the level of the galactosphere, it is the core that generates so much energy that most of the intergalactic electromagnetic energies are filtered out. The Milky Way has its very own sphere of influence. At that level, the frequencies from outside the sphere that penetrate it are also part of the evolutionary process of the entire galactosphere, the heliosphere and the geosphere. The electric ecosystem extends deep into the galactosphere. While the galactosphere continues its journey through the universe, it tries to keep its very own nature intact, but also exposes itself in the meantime to new forces in its path which may change and develop the whole of its being. That which it cannot keep out will have to be processed inside the whole of the galactosphere. In other words, in derived form we experience the very things the Milky Way experiences. This is how this new spheric frame of reference develops and grows.

Everywhere, at every level of electromagnetic manifestation, the unique character of the prevailing sphere becomes visible. Those levels also play themselves out in us, at a psychological, mental, or emotional level, because in derived form their electromagnetic influences rain down on our roads and streets, right through the roofs of our houses every day and without us realizing it. It may be a source of consternation in our lives when those influences are ignored, and levels get mixed up.

By separating processes and getting to know energy types, we travel along in spheres within spheres within spheres.

Electrospheric developments: living in a fish in a fish in a fish

These spheric insights have a conclusion as simple as it is inevitable: we are all part of it. Something considers life on earth so important that neither trouble nor expense is spared in wrapping all life forms carefully in spheres, membrane after membrane, layer after layer, cortex after cortex.

The idea of being a neutral observer becomes problematic because we simply live IN something. We live IN a geospheric field rotating IN a heliospheric field, which in turn rotates IN a galactospheric field. We do not have to look for something outside of ourselves, because the huge boundlessness of space is just as much IN us as outside of us.

Through this ordering of ourselves and of the universe we participate in everything, are present at everything and in the middle of everything. This can be illustrated by a possibly somewhat strange analogy: 'the inception bomb shot'. This is a large glass of orange juice, inside which is a smaller glass of beer which, in turn, contains an even smaller glass with, for example, Jägermeister. A glass in a glass in a glass. The orange juice constantly mixes with the beer and the Jägermeister.

In essence, every influence of all higher spheres can be felt and measured here on earth. Each cell in our body reflects the potency of all functions in the whole body. The human may be a minute cell in the body of the galactosphere, nevertheless it reflects all its possibilities.

The fact that cells have specialised does not change their dedication to all functions. The air we breathe is the same air as the pharaohs breathed. And the water we drink is the same water the ancient Chinese and ancient Romans drank. Yet both air and water have changed and evolved under the influence of the spheric context. Why would we then look at the sun as if it were far way, while we live inside the charisma of the solar heliosphere where neutrinos pass through our body every second of every day? At a semiconscious and unconscious level, our body is much more intelligent than we are. On a continuous basis it maintains interactive contact with what currently happens in the heliosphere.

The spheric context in which de geosphere lives like a fish in a fish in a fish

Is the idea so unthinkable that some of the most beautiful, most original and most innovative fruits in human history in art, literature and science are a certain form of translation of that mysterious connection with the heliosphere? Is it unthinkable that even more refined and sophisticated forms of creativity, inspiration and genius in the fields of architecture, such as the pyramids, and in music and religion originate in the translation of interstellar particles from the galactosphere, in which we as a species have already been travelling for millennia? Everything that happens to the galactosphere or the heliosphere also happens to us. The transfer for participation is immediate.

Spheric development

Could it be that the spheres together point to a way of personal growth and evolution, in which they are like an external mirror to us for an internal development stage?

Does the moon reflect a childlike stage full of new possibilities – lack of organic life, the urge to learn, need for leadership and support, need for radiance and charisma? Does the moon embody the stage of our childhood and all that this entails?

When we look at the earth and the geomagnetic sphere, does it reflect our own ability to develop an atmosphere and charisma, the ability to form our own organic life and our own consciousness? Do we see within the geomagnetic field a reflection of the huge variety of skills, functions, abilities and craftsmanship with the associated qualities that can be learned?

Perhaps the sun and its heliosphere can inspire us to leadership and to give light, to give protection, to take up responsibilities? Maybe tuning to the heliosphere gives us the courage to let others temporarily hide under our wings? So what does the galactosphere reflect when we look in its mirror?

Spheric context

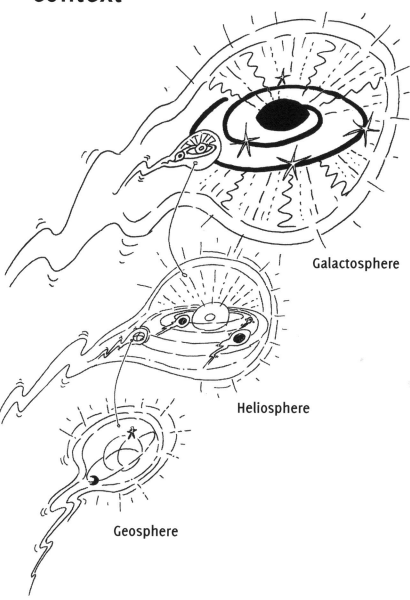

Galactosphere

Heliosphere

Geosphere

Birds

Googling nightingales, charged hummingbirds and robins with virtual reality glasses

It is important for us to become aware of the ecosystem's sensitivity for radiation frequencies. All things living in the ecosystem work with that sensitivity. Birds are physically responsive to different types of electricity and magnetism.

Positively charged birds and negatively charged flowers

As we have seen in the chapter on honeybees, electrical phenomena can play an important role in pollinating flowers. Now it turns out that birds also have a role to play here. By rubbing their wings against flower petals and moving them rapidly in the charged open air, the static electric charge, of for example hummingbirds, increases. Hummingbirds can carry charges up to 800 picocoulombs. An electrically positively charged hummingbird attracts electrically negatively charged flower spores. Due to the reversal of the charge, these birds also appear to help with pollination [1*]. It is a dance of attraction and repulsion. In the process, everything revolves around electromagnetic sensitivity. The entire ecosystem seems imbued with this.

Navigating on the earth's magnetic field using the magnetic sense

Animals make use of specific electromagnetically collected and stored intelligence from the geomagnetic field to plan their migration routes and 'google restaurants' for the trip. For example, nightingales plan their entire migration routes using the geomagnetic field. Until 2001, people had no idea whatsoever why birds would take a foraging break in a particular country and in a particular region and then spend the night there. But after all, the animals need to eat and rest as well as fly. Thanks to rings around their legs, scientists knew that the nightingales departing from Sweden dined and rested in northern Egypt. This is essential, because they then fly 1,500 kilometres across the Sahara desert without any stops to arrive at their final hibernation site in Central Africa. A number of nightingales which were about to make their first south-bound migration were captured by the researchers and placed in the midst of four magnetic coils to simulate both the strength and the direction of the magnetic field. Some of these nightingales were exposed to Sweden's magnetic field, while the rest were exposed to the strength and direction of Egypt's magnetic field. Compared to the Swedish situation, both the power and the slope angle of the magnetic field were decreased. As a result, the birds in the imitated Egyptian field began to eat like there was no tomorrow. Nobody understands precisely how the magnetic stimuli of the geomagnetic field directs the hypothalamus of the migrating nightingale so the bird will eat exactly in northern Egypt. A distinct nerve receptor has not been found yet. Only the bobolink, a large North American meadow bird, developed a potential difference in the fibres of the trigeminal nerve, a nerve which runs above the beak to the brain. This potential difference arose when it was exposed to a change in the magnetic field. The researchers were faced with a mystery: the magnetic sensitivity must be an inborn characteristic, because the first-year nightingales had never been in Egypt before [2*].

Looking at these types of naturally built-in abilities, society has identified natural electromagnetic sensitivities as highly sensitive or hypersensitive. This is a peculiar description, because sensitivity has to do with simply participating in certain natural aspects of life that are generally accessible to animals and plants, but that are not yet so generally accessible to most humans. The said research into nightingales, and also research into birds such as pigeons and waders, seems to indicate that electromagnetic sensitivity within the ecosystem is a condition for life. Becoming sensitive is therefore not a high goal or a hyper-defect. Our bodies seem to be just as sensitive as those of animals. The only step that might be missing is to start doing something with it. This is not an option for animals. They use that sensitivity on a continuous basis.

Not just sensing but also seeing the geomagnetic field

While humans have three types of cones in their retina that are sensitive to three different regions of the colour spectrum, birds have at least four types of cones which enable them to see the radiation of ultraviolet light in addition to ordinary light [3*].

A 2009 research revealed the electroreception of birds. This is in addition to the way in which birds sometimes use their beaks as electromagnetic equipment to maintain contact with the geomagnetic field. Electroreception means that in this case birds can see the geomagnetic field directly with their eyes. The robins in the research appear able to literally see the magnetic field of the earth and the entire electromagnetic dynamics that are going on in it. To this end, they use a part of the brain known as cluster N, a region that enables birds to decipher complex electromagnetic signals. This specific region of the brain is receiving its information from certain photopigments in the eye of the bird. This allows the animal to record the direction, power and inclination of the geomagnetic field [4*].

The earth's magnetic field is currently very weak and is weakening further every year. It becomes therefore increasingly difficult to detect. Measured at the surface of the earth, the field currently appears to be between 30 and 65 microtesla. This is a fraction of the power of a whiteboard magnet. How is it possible that robins and other animals can tune so accurately to such a weak influence? The only thing you can get moving with this weak influence is the needle of a compass. The key appears to be in eye protein, the so-called cryptochrome. By using it, robins, fruit flies and other animals appear to have the ability to visualise different facets of the geomagnetic field [5*].

 ## The impact of artificial EMFs on birds

In order to see whether artificial EMFs could disturb these geo-sensitive abilities of robins, a group of researchers waited for the robins to migrate south in the autumn. They then put the birds in Emlen funnels, spaces that can register the preferred direction of the birds when they try to escape. Inside those spaces, the robins were then exposed to different oscillating magnetic fields and they were observed to see if those fields disturbed the natural sense of orientation. To the astonishment of the researchers, a magnetic field tuned to 1.3 MHz proved to be one of the things that could disturb the robins' sense of orientation. When the frequency of the field increased or when it decreased, the interference had less impact [6*].

By refining and extending the measurements, it was found that more artificial EMFs could disturb the natural sense of orientation and inclination compass of the robins. In the years following, the research was expanded to include the sensitivity of other birds for artificial EMFs. Here are four examples.

I Storks - Electromagnetic signals from transmission masts have a negative effect on white stork populations. Observations of a stork population in the vicinity of transmission masts were carried out in Valladolid, Spain. Very significant differences were found between the total productivity of the nests at 200 metres and the ones at more than 300 metres distance from the masts. In another intensive research, fruitless attemps by storks to reproduce in nests near transmission masts were observed. Some pairs of birds were unable to build their nests and other pairs fought with each other. These results demonstrate that signals from transmission masts have a negative effect on the reproductivity of white storks [7*].

I Garden warblers - Artificially induced magnetic radiation at the bandwidth of 1.4 MHz causes disorientation of the natural sense of navigation and sense of direction of garden warblers [8*].

I Migratory birds become disoriented above towns - Artificially induced high-frequency electromagnetic radiation at the bandwidth of 50 KHz and 5 MHz disrupts the natural sense of navigation and sense of direction of migratory birds. Whenever these birds fly across towns and villages, they appear to become most disorientated [9*].

I Birds disappear from Greece - A Greek research shows that with each new generation of transmission masts more birds disappear from the Greek landscape [10*].

The unknown life of chickens

Chickens detect magnetic fields, too. Like robins, they do not do this by using magnetite crystals in their beak, but directly with their eyes. Under the influence of light, it seems that free radicals are released in their eye pigment that can be influenced by magnetic fields. It means that chickens, compared to us, see very different things. Their field of vision is expanded with an additional magnetic dimension [11*].

Chickens can see magnetic fields

So, chickens are clairvoyant in a special way. They probably see shapes, colours, dynamics and magnetic densities, which for most people can only be approached theoretically and empirically. Chickens may not be migratory birds, but it is known they are still able to orientate on the geomagnetic field. But we must assume that chickens may also be able to perceive other magnetic phenomena, such as the magnetic fields around power lines or lamps. We do not have the faintest idea about the function or purpose of the additional sensory abilities of these birds.

Gradually, the chicken has become merely a product in a multi-million dollar industry. In the Netherlands, approximately 100 million chickens are kept by 1,500 farms. That is approximately 65,000 birds per farm. Every chicken has a life that is not understood at all at the moment. They see things, respond to things and possibly feel things that lie outside people's frame of reference. The effect of magnetoreception on animals is unknown. Because there is no familiarity with what chickens see and experience, people come up with solutions that may serve economic interests, but do not meet the problems arising from the experiences of chickens. If chickens might panic from artificial magnetic fields surrounding them in the shed, for example, then the question is whether a (metal) pair of chicken glasses is such a good solution. After all, social stress among these birds can easily be seen, but inner stress in chickens is hard to detect. Clearly, these are considerations for further research.

Only by putting ourselves in the natural ways in which animals and plants are electromagnetically entangled, can we build sufficient understanding for the way in which they experience things. By experimenting with electroreception and magnetoreception ourselves, we may be able to understand a little bit better what happens to animals. It seems that the only way to understand sensitivity in other life forms is for humans to develop their own sensitivity.

Female zebra finches look at the radiation of males

Knots do not have to do any systematic digging or burrowing to find their food. They find it by using a sensitive organ that can detect frequencies of small prey animals under the sand [12*]. So one peck and it is dinner time.

What seems to us to be a strange gift is for animals simply a form of electroreception or an ability to specifically google the geomagnetic field. Female zebra finches possess a very special form of electroreception which has not been mentioned before. When choosing their partners they mainly look at the ultraviolet radiation of the males. Researchers have demonstrated that when the female can only see the males through a filter that blocks UV light, she does not show any interest in the opposite sex. Birds of prey make use of their ability to detect their prey in the presence of UV light. And how is it that blackbirds can accurately trace worms hidden in the ground? [13*]

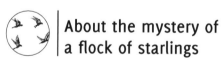 ## About the mystery of a flock of starlings

Many phenomena, such as the extraordinary orchestration and the magnificent choreography of a flight of birds, do not seem to be really understood without considering the geomagnetic entanglement. Just as we have seen with the beautiful shapes a bacterial colony can make, we can see that almost mathematical beauty again in a flock of starlings that fly across the country in a dynamic that changes form endlessly.

A single flock can contain more than 60,000 starlings. There are a number of current views about the reason for this choreography in the air. Is it just a way to indicate the new place to sleep or is it related to food? This has been a mystery for a very long time. Perhaps it is time to research whether the magnetic field of the earth has anything to do with it? In 2016, researcher Chiu Fan Lee from Imperial College, London, linked the way in which, for example, grasshoppers, bacteria, schools of fish, human cells and starlings can pattern their movement to a known source: the magnet.

Could the geomagnetic field be the influence inspiring the next starling murmuration? If more indications could be found to support this, then what kind of electromagnetic phenomena do birds react to? Where does the intelligence live that causes the shapes that starlings make together?

Birds that Google

Hummingbirds pollinate flowers through a process of electrical charging and electrical discharging

With their beaks as antennae, birds detect small prey under the sand

Under the influence of transmission masts, storks struggle to reproduce and garden warblers become disorientated

Female zebra finches mainly look at the radiation of the males when choosing their partner

Nightingales plan their migration route using the geomagnetic field

Hummingbirds charge their bodies like a battery during flight

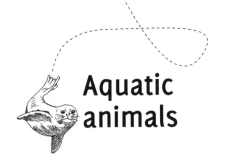

Aquatic animals

How sharks can smell electrons and how seals make use of a radar moustache

The concepts of intelligence and consciousness are often used interchangeably. For the purpose of this chapter on aquatic animals we separate these two for a moment to illustrate something. Aquatic animals are intelligent; they make use of electroreception and magnetoreception. They are, however, not conscious of this. As is the case with bacteria and birds, for example, electroreception and magnetoreception are not only abilities of the individual animal. These abilities connect the animal with a geospheric intelligence.

Electroreception enables bees, sharks, cockroaches, anteaters, rays and platypuses to see right through an obstacle [1*]. They can perceive electrical impulses freely everywhere, even if physical obstacles obstruct sight. That is an intelligent ability. It seems to be up to the animals themselves to do what they want with those observations. But also with aquatic animals we will see that the way they are entangled with the earth's magnetic field gives them an intelligence, which means they no longer act or react as separate animals. The 'apps' with which they are connected to the geomagnetic internet offer amazing advantages; advantages they respond to and live with, but without being conscious of them.

Electroreception and electrolocation in sharks and rays

Sharks and rays use electroreception and electrolocation to explore the earth's magnetic field in ways humans can only dream of. Sharks have sensitive faculties you would not expect. They can smell electrons many kilometres away. What does that mean? Sharks possess a very sensitive detection mechanism for electric fields. This allows them to register the extremely weak fields produced by the body cells of other fish. In addition, they can also use the weak magnetic fields of the earth to determine their position.

The sense for registering electricity works under conditions where the remaining senses are virtually unusable, such as in pitch black and turbid water or if a prey is hiding under the sand or behind a stone. Measurements of brain reactions suggest that a shark can distinguish even a fraction of a volt, a field strength in seawater that technicians equipped with the most modern measuring devices can barely measure. This is how sensitive sharks are. They can detect and use impulses as a kind of radar system, but do not seem capable of producing electricity themselves [2*]. In addition to this electric ability, sharks also possess a more magnetic side, which means they always live in entanglement with the geospheric field which tells them where they are located.

There is growing evidence that biological cells in the body of a living organism act as a battery. The bodies of fish in seawater, for instance, act as a battery that is usually activated and spreads a continuous electric field around it. When a fish pumps water through its gills, this field changes. In order to distinguish these very subtle fields in seawater from other aquatic animals, from each other and from the earth's magnetic field, sharks have thousands of specialized detectors in their snouts, called ampullae of Lorenzini. These ampullae are covered with a single layer of sensory cells that activate the nearby nerves. These then inform the brain when there is an electric field and from which fish it originates [3*, 4*].

Shocking
bony fish

Some 300 species of bony fish have been identified, which, like sharks and rays, also have the ability of electroreception. Unlike sharks, some bony fish do produce electric charges themselves. The electric eel, for instance, can navigate through muddy waters by continuously emitting electrical impulses. The eel uses this to register how the impulses reflect back from stones and other objects. This is how the fish translates the signals from its surroundings. The potency of this ability is probably so strong in fish because water conducts electricity much better than air. The electric eel itself can produce shocks of over 600 volts. The required organs for this are located in the cells of the tail muscles. These cells act like batteries by storing massive charges and then discharging them outright in one go, if required. Electric rays, some catfish and electric eels, use these built-in electroshock weapons to paralyse, stun or kill prey fish, but they also use this weapon to protect themselves [5*].

What elephant nose fish
have in common with robins

In the many inland lakes and rivers of Africa an enormous number of whispers can be heard, inaudible to the human ear. It resembles the murmur of a busy underwater marketplace. This is where the elephant nose fish meet. They owe their name to their trunks. This fish species can produce and detect electric fields. Elephant nose fish use their gift to navigate through turbid water, hunt down their prey and communicate with each other. There are more than 200 species of elephant nose fish that all speak to each other in their own electromagnetic dialect. When looking for a suitable partner, these fish literally watch their radiation first [6*].

Elephant nose fish communicate by means of EMFs and maintain a mutual difference of 10 to 15 Hz to avoid interference with each other's frequencies. When looking for a suitable partner, elephant nose fish watch their radiation

They communicate by means of EMST. These are electrical organ discharges of 1 KHz. The fish can perceive frequencies of just a millionth of a second. By changing these frequencies and the type of impulse, the elephant nose fish can exchange information among themselves about sex, location, distance, social status, sexual readiness, and so forth. The signals they send out are possibly even converted into songs which they use to serenade potential partners. If the discharge frequencies of two elephant nose fish become too similar, they increase the frequency distance. Fish in schools maintain a mutual difference of 10 to 15 Hz [7*, 8*].

They also use their EMST to collaborate and warn each other about predatory attacks. A large part of their brains is dedicated to communication by means of electroreception and EMST.

The geospheric entanglement of the salmon

The chapter on 'Higher Spheres' describes how the sun's electrical activities and the way the earth's magnetic field reacts to sperm whales have an impact on the navigation abilities of these whales [9*].

Like sharks, eels and tunas, salmon use the geomagnetic field of the earth intensively to navigate and cover long distances. The mechanism responsible for this operates at cellular level. Some cells in the salmon contain the famous magnetite crystals that create a cellular compass. By studying trout, which anatomically resemble salmon, researchers found swirling cells, cells that rotate. The magnetic particles are stuck to the cell membrane and because they are constantly drawn to the lines of the earth's geomagnetic field, they exert certain forces on the cell membrane when the salmon deviates from its path through the water [10*].

This way salmon are constantly experiencing the forces of the geomagnetic field first-hand. These forces dictate direction. Salmon therefore have no choice but to be an extension of the intelligence of geomagnetic force fields. The downside is that it also makes them sensitive to artificial EMFs. A 1980 study demonstrated that salmon and eels suffer from heart rhythm disorders as a result of exposure to specific artificial frequencies [11*]. In the years following 1980, more research was done into the effects of exposure to artificial EMFs on fish. Here are a few examples.

I Trout - Exposure of trout to an artificial magnetic field slows down the embryonic development of this fish. Magnetic fields can also be the cause of changes in the blood circulation of pike, carp and trout. The magnetic fields increase the breathing intensity of trout. The fish's sense of direction appears to be controlled by the natural earth's magnetic field but can also be disorientated by artificially created magnetic fields [12*].

I Zebrafish - Exposing zebrafish with embryos to artificial low-frequency magnetic fields has adverse effects on the embryonic development of the zebrafish. This exposure gives a negative influence on breeding because its heart rate lowers, and it causes apoptosis. Although such effects do not pose an immediate lethal threat to the zebrafish, it can nevertheless be concluded that they are very stressed [13*].

I Sea urchins - Under the influence of artificial EMFs several abnormalities in embryonic development were observed in sea urchins [14*].

I Eels - The effect of undersea alternating current cables on eels in the Baltic Sea: sixty eels were tagged and their migration speed was measured in an area where a 130 kilovolt alternating current cable was located. The eels' swimming speed was significantly lower around the power cable [15*].

Further examples of the possible impact of exposure to artificial EMFs on the natural functioning of aquatic animals can be found in the chapter on consequences for animals and plants.

 ## Seals with a radar moustache

For human beings, active connection to the earth's magnetic field is at best only a vague collective memory of folkloristic and mythical times. Just picture, for example, what a wonderful story it would be to tell about a man with a radar moustache, someone who could scan strangers with his moustache without having to talk to them. Maybe this is nonsense, but it could well become an evocative story if it was well written and told, and especially if you had a moustache that could do such a thing. Seals do have such a moustache. They use their whiskers as an electromagnetic radar system to detect movements in their environment. They are so good at it that they hardly need eyes. Blind seals are able to by-pass objects unerringly. The animals move their moustache back and forth as a fan and are therefore able to detect and follow a prey from a great distance. Each of their whiskers is connected to some 1,600 nerve cells. By swinging and twisting their heads, they constantly scan their surroundings with their ultra-sensitive whiskers, which tell them much more about their surroundings than their large ink-black eyes. Seals' whiskers are 10 times more sensitive than cats' whiskers [16*]. Of course, the question arises whether men could learn to perceive so sharply with their moustache or beard?

Sea turtels with a GPS

Researchers discovered that young loggerhead sea turtles use the geosphere as their navigation system. They swim on their own from Florida to West Africa, a 12,900-kilometre journey with numerous dangers that takes them 5 to 10 years to complete. In their route around the Atlantic Ocean, they skilfully navigate through deadly cold waters, for example. It is astonishing to realise that they make that journey all by themselves. Young turtles do not follow older turtles; they navigate alone. In the experiment, young turtles were placed in a water tank and coils were used to generate the exact magnetic fields that the animals would encounter along the way. The turtles navigated on the magnetic fields as if they had a GPS. This ability also explains why adult animals find their way back to the breeding ground. Experiments with these artificial magnetic fields demonstrate that the animals have the ability to register the direction and strength of the earth's magnetic field [17*]. This is how sea turtles were added to the arsenal of animals that have all kinds of mysterious sensitivities to the earth's geosphere. In the animals studied, scientists repeatedly found those pieces of magnetite which seem to be able to serve as a mobile phone, a GPS and the like.

Squids with a 'Klingon cloaking device'

It is miraculous to see the arms of a squid at work with their strength and flexibility. They move effortlessly like underwater dancers in a spontaneous choreography of ever-changing patterns against the clear blue background of the salty seawater. How is it possible that they can have all these different tentacles perform all kinds of graceful, complementary actions without getting caught up for one single moment?

Humans and monkey species are limited in their movements by hinges, such as elbows, wrist or shoulder joints. These joints also give some control and make some of the movements controllable. But where is the squids' control system to coordinate this unlimited freedom of movement? Initially it was assumed that the central brain in the head of squids arranged the entire control of the tentacles. Hence the Greek name *Cephalopoda*, which literally means 'head-footed'.

Squids can conceal their electrical signals like the Klingons in Star Trek

Because the squids' arms are placed in a circle around their heads, it was assumed that the head was the centre of all their antics. This turns out not to be the case. The central brain of the squid directs only the gross motor skills by means of electrical signals via the nerve bundles. The fine motor skills are arranged by separate nerve centres in each of the arms. So, the arms have a certain autonomy and improvise on the larger choreographic themes indicated by the squid's brain. The central coordination of the brain determines the rhythm and each of the legs improvises on it. The octopus is a wonderful life form with 9 brains, 3 hearts and... blue blood [18*, 19*]

The refined communication between the input from the head and the improvisations by the tentacles is so important that the squid has a 'back-up' intranet to be able to continue the exchange of electrical signals at all times. For example, if a squid becomes entangled in a net and the nerve bundles between the central brain and the tentacles are damaged or even cut through, the contact between the brain and the arms is immediately taken over by another network. The squid brain then uses its skin to stay in touch with the arms by means of electrical signals. This magnificent underwater dancer appears to be a stronghold of two types of internal electromagnetic communication [20*].

Squids can also conceal their electrical signals; just like the Klingons in Star Trek, they have a *cloaking device*. In the event of imminent danger from sharks, for example, squids can immediately dim the electric fields they usually emit [21*], making it difficult for sharks to locate them. So, under the most precarious conditions, the squids can continue their underwater dance because of their electric camouflage techniques and their double intranet, making them almost unstoppable.

Because the understandings relating to all electric abilities of squids and other aquatic animals are based on recent discoveries, it is difficult to predict what the ever-increasing presence of power cables and electromagnetic radiation in the oceans will cause. Saltwater is ideally suited for conductivity. What is the influence that artificial EMFs have on the underwater ecosystem?

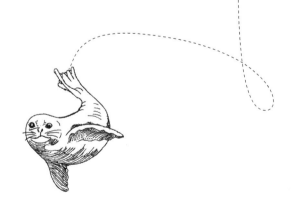

Shocking fish

Elephant nose fish communicate by means of EMFs and maintain a mutual difference of 10 to 15 Hz to avoid interference with each other's frequencies. When looking for a suitable partner, elephant nose fish watch their radiation

The electric eel can give shocks of over 600 volts. The required organs are located in the cells of the tail muscles. These cells act like batteries and can store massive charges that may suddenly be discharged again in a single shock

Sperm whales react to solar activity. Artificial EMFs cause embryonic abnormalities in sea urchins. The snout of sharks is ultra-electro-receptive

Loggerhead sea turtles swim from Florida to West Africa, using only the geosphere as their navigation system

Seals use their whiskers as radar system

Frogs

In 1791, there was a dead frog on the table in Luigi Galvani's back garden. Metal wires connected a lightning rod to the lifeless animal. Then came the storm and lightning flashed down the wires to the frog. The frog's legs contracted, twitched. Here was the evidence for a connection between electricity and movement. Galvani believed he had found the key to life by exposing the relationship between electricity and movement in organic material. Later, through a series of experiments, he would adequately prove that there is such a thing as internal, animal electricity [1*]. It is strange that a truth that has been known for more than 200 years has never really been placed in context. That is to say, the context that everything works by electricity and magnetism. Or is it perhaps because the electromagnetic processes in biological material are difficult to categorise?

At the end of 2000, the Ig Nobel Prize was awarded to Andre Geim. He appeared in the news with experiments in which he let a living clawed frog float in a magnetic field after he had seen that liquids in superstrong magnetic fields sometimes start to float just like that. This floating was possible because magnetic fields and electric currents are interrelated. A coil through which current flows will generate a magnetic field and, in turn, a moving magnetic field will cause an electric current. Now, the thing is that certain substances, such as water, have a property called diamagnetism. A frog, like most animals, consists for the most part of water. The animal appears to have similar diamagnetic properties to water. Some materials, such as iron, are known for their magnetic properties. Frogs are not. Then how can they float in a magnetic field?

If a frog, which is made up of a lot of water, is placed in a strong magnetic field, a magnetic field inside the animal will emerge that is opposite to the external magnetic field. This means that the field inside the frog and the external magnetic field repel each other, causing the frog to float. Thanks to the properties of superconductivity, it is possible to generate a magnetic field that is strong enough to achieve this. Research is now being carried out into the possibility of trains floating with the aid of magnetic fields. Only superior conductivity can generate fields strong enough to keep a train in the air.

Like all other aspects of the organic and inorganic ecosystem, frogs are made up of countless atoms. Each of these atoms contains electrons that orbit around a central core. But when atoms are in a powerful magnetic field, the electrons change their orbits in the atom. The atoms get their own magnetic sphere because of these shifts. When a frog is placed in a very powerful magnetic field, its composition changes. The frog is no longer made up of neutral atoms, but essentially of numerous small magnets. It becomes diamagnetic [2*].

As stated, all things, including water, bacteria, mushrooms and also people, are basically diamagnetic. Just as levitation is possible for frogs, potentially the same could be possible for a stadium full of football supporters, an elephant or a cheese sandwich. When this mechanism began to be understood, it might have been possible for scientists to dig deeper instead of dismissing this discovery by awarding a prize for ridiculous research. Ig Nobel is a play on words on Alfred Nobel's name. By turning the English word noble into ignoble, it is in fact denying that this is a noble or interesting research. The prize is a parody of the Nobel Prize and is awarded one week before the announcement of the real Nobel Prize winners to ten studies conducted that made people laugh at first but were subsequently thought-provoking. Geim's research certainly deserves the latter. After all, all life takes place on an immense, planetary magnet with an even larger magnetic field. What if the conditions on earth changed and the magnetic forces completely or partially eliminated the laws of gravity? What might that cause? What more could there be floating along?

Frogs have all kinds of hidden electromagnetic properties. Unfortunately, many of these properties come to light by antagonizing, confusing, hindering or disorienting animals rather than by looking at them and putting ourselves in their place. One study as an example found indications for the direct influence of artificially generated magnetic fields on frogs. The growth of leopard frog embryos, for example, was severely restricted by placing them in a highly fluctuating magnetic field [3*].

 ## Consequences of low-frequency radiation for frogs

In 2018, researchers succeeded in extracting energy from frog eggs to charge a condenser which could produce a radio signal. The researchers managed to have the frogs' eggs produce 1.1 nanowatt of power [4*]. During the growth and development process, most embryos generate observable electric fields. These fields prove to be important for shaping such things as the tail structure in chickens and the overall development of salamanders, but also the left-right asymmetry in frogs [5*].

By understanding that so many aspects of the life of frogs are determined and influenced by electricity and magnetism, might we be more cautious in increasing the use of artificial EMFs? For example, if the knowledge were widely supported that prolonged exposure of tadpoles to a weak magnetic 50 Hz field is almost, but not completely, lethal to them, we might ask ourselves what effect the huge magnetic fields from power pylons in nature reserves have on the lives of frogs and other animals. And if we were to accept the research results showing that a weak magnetic 50 Hz field inhibits the growth and developmental rate of tadpoles and slows down their process of metamorphosis [6*], we might seriously consider taking frogs into account by earthing the high-voltage cables more thoroughly or by diverting them around areas where many of these animals live. Is there a way to ensure that we handle our artificial energy demand in such a manner that the natural electromagnetic systems of frogs and other animals remain intact?

Consequences of high-frequency radiation for frogs

After mobile phone transmission masts and transmitting equipment for 15 television channels were installed in the Nardi area of a national park in Australia, scientists and park keepers witnessed an exodus of animals. 27 bird species disappeared, and the insect population declined dramatically in volume. When the system was expanded with newer transmission technologies in 2013, the exodus increased: 49 bird species disappeared, bats became scarce, species of moths and butterflies vanished, the natural population of toads and frogs in the area decreased dramatically and several species of ants became rare. Furthermore, some animals showed unnatural behaviour [7*].

The results of another study, in which the eggs of frogs were exposed to electromagnetic radiation from various transmission masts at a distance of 140 metres, eventually led to deficient coordination of movement, growth disorders and a very high mortality rate of 90% among the tadpoles. In the control group, under identical circumstances, the movement coordination was normal, the development synchronous and the mortality rate merely 4.2%. These results show that the radiation emitted by masts has serious consequences for the health and life expectancy of frogs [8*].

Floating Frogs

Exposure of frog eggs to high-frequency radiation led to deficient coordination of movement, growth disorders and a very high mortality rate of 90% among the tadpoles

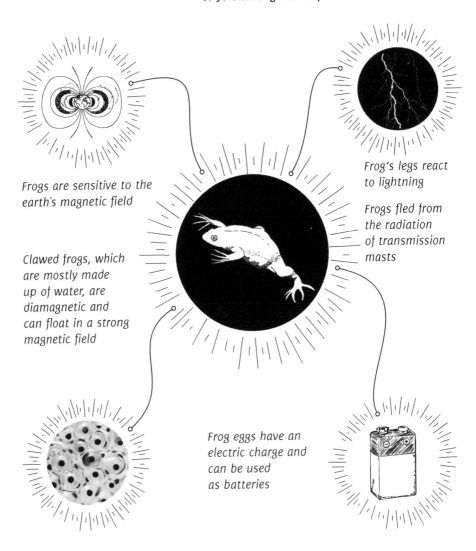

Frogs are sensitive to the earth's magnetic field

Clawed frogs, which are mostly made up of water, are diamagnetic and can float in a strong magnetic field

Frog's legs react to lightning

Frogs fled from the radiation of transmission masts

Frog eggs have an electric charge and can be used as batteries

Plants

How plants make use of a wired internal nervous system and how they can warn each other with electrical signals

Electric charge is everywhere around us. The atmosphere is full of it. Every raindrop and every snowflake that falls has an electric charge [1,2]. In a forest, the electrical composition of the air differs from that in a city. That is why these places cause different feelings. It is not difficult to experience for yourself how important it is that the air quality remains enriched with ions. In the mountains and by the sea this is naturally the case, and the air has a quality ranging between 2,000 and 5,000 ions per cubic centimetre. Most of these ions have a negative charge. In a city, the concentration of ions quickly drops far below 1,000 ions per cubic centimetre. The positive ions then get the upper hand. The natural ratio between positive and negative ions on earth is 2:3. So there is always a natural surplus of negative oxygen ions. Clean air contains about 66 percent nitrogen and about 33 percent oxygen and is filled with positively and negatively charged ions. As soon as the 2:3 ion ratio changes, how-ever, this also has negative health effects on people, animals and plants. Of course, the total ion density is important too [3].

How trees charge the atmosphere

Electric charges in the atmosphere are constantly formed by all kinds of natural sources: the sun, the wind, the rain, lightning, the earth and the trees. Plants and trees are not only the lungs of the planet, but also play a role in electrically charging the atmosphere. The positive and negative ion concentrations above forests are twice as high compared to grasslands, for example. Ions can also be released into the air by natural EMFs from space and by radon gas from the earth's surface. Trees appear to function like some kind of radon pump. They extract the gas from the soil through their roots and then release it into the atmosphere through their leaves. This is especially true of trees with deep roots, such as eucalyptuses, which contribute to the electrification of the atmosphere. And charged or ionized, particles are held much better by the lungs than uncharged particles [4*].

The more negative ions the air contains, the fresher the air becomes. At a waterfall in a forest, the ion concentration in the air can rise to more than 10,000 ions per cubic centimetre, while in an old, poorly ventilated office in the middle of the city the ion concentration can drop to as little as 50 ions per cubic centimetre. In addition, the negative ions will prevail at a waterfall, while the positive ions will prevail in that stuffy office.

As we saw in the introduction, there is a fundamental difference between the electricity that energizes our bodies and the electricity we use to light our cities at night. The electricity in the wiring in walls is carried by fast electrons, while the slow electricity passing through the plant and animal kingdom is carried by ions. An electric signal through a wire travels almost at the speed of light, while the fastest nerve impulses travel at about 0.12 kilometres per second [5*]. That 0.12 kilometres per second is still 4,320 kilometres per hour or four times the speed of an airplane.

The ion-based life of plants is so strong that people can tap it. If you stick an electrode into a tree and a second electrode into the surrounding soil, for example, a weak electric current can be tapped from the tree. The difference in pH value between the tree and the soil accounts for the potential difference. The voltage provided by a tree ranges from 20 millivolts to several hundred millivolts [6*]. In the last ten years, all kinds of economic applications have been devised for harvesting electricity from plants. In 2019, the start-up business Plant-e reported that a football field with wet grass can provide electricity to ten households. That is wonderful. Perhaps it would be wiser and also fascinating to first find out a little more about the way in which the electric world of plants works. Why do flowers and trees actually need this steady flow of slow ions and impulses? Will the charge or the signal function of this ion flow change by tapping it or exposing it to artificial EMFs, for example? The truth is, no one really knows at the moment.

 ## Floating pollen and electrically charged cobwebs

Negative ions enter the atmosphere because the earth itself, as we have seen, has a negative charge relative to the ionosphere. This causes other negative produced ions to be repelled, such as the negative ions that occur at a waterfall, in evaporating water, snow, a shower of rain, hail, and trees. A giant magnet was required to make a little creature like a frog float. But what about pollen? Many phenomena can be explained by establishing a link between the ecosystem and electricity. The chapter on bees, for example, describes how these insects build up positive charges and flowers negative ones. We have also seen how bees can distinguish different floral frequencies by means of electroreception, and we have established that the difference in voltage between flowers and bees is the result of the positively charged geomagnetic field that causes bees to have a positive charge, and the negatively charged earth that causes plants to build up a negative charge. The soil, the trees and the plants as well as the animals are constantly being charged negatively, while bees build up a positive charge. Electric charges from plants (negative) and pollinators, such as bees (positive), are believed to promote pollination by enabling pollen grains to jump from flowers to pollinators and vice versa. We have seen that pollen not only floats back and forth between bees and plants, but also between hummingbirds and plants. What about trees fertilized by the wind?

The sun bombards the earth's atmosphere with large positively charged protons, charging the atmosphere. In addition, a constant flow of small, fast, negatively charged electrons is reaching the earth's surface. Therefore, the earth is negatively charged and the atmosphere positive. Through trees, the atmosphere can naturally discharge itself again and again. A tree in bloom expels negatively charged pollen at a temperature of 17 degrees Celsius. Actually, this pollen would be pulled down by gravity, but because it is repelled by the earth's negative charge, the pollen remains floating at the same height above the ground: pollen levitation. This is the ideal height to fertilise the surrounding trees. In this way, it is possible to direct floating particles along their path through the air using electrical signals [7*]. In reality, they are not wind-fertilized trees at all. They are rather plants that practise 'electroportation' of pollen.

Spiders use the same principle to catch insects. Biologists have discovered that charged prey significantly improves the success of cobwebs. If you rub a balloon against your hair, some electrons get stuck to the balloon, keeping your hair positively charged. The same is true of flying insects. Like bees, other flying insects build up a positive electric charge because of the constant friction that occurs between the wings and the air particles while flying. Most plants carry a negative charge.

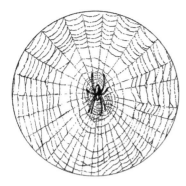

Spiders catch positively charged insects with a negatively charged spider web

Because spiders often attach their cobwebs to plants, cobwebs also have a negative charge. The positively charged flying insects are thus attracted by the negatively charged cobwebs [8*]. Flies and the like are, as it were, 'electroported' to the spider's web.

 ## The difference between atoms and ions

An atom is like a miniature solar system with a nucleus playing the part of the sun. The electrons swirl like planets around the nucleus. Just like in the solar system where the sun is in fact a minuscule dust particle in proportion to the distance at which the planets orbit, the nucleus of the atom is minuscule in proportion to the distance of the whirling electrons. If you were to remove all space from all atoms, the world and everything that lives on it would take up no more space than the volume of a small potato or a radish. Space contains remarkably little mass. The universe is essentially 99% empty, at least if you only search for substance and matter. What then is the miraculous energy that organises the scarce matter in such a way that a rose or a pine tree can manifest in all the whirling of the electrons?

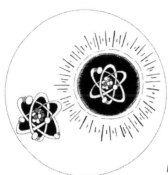

How an atom becomes an ion

Under normal circumstances, the charge of an atom is neutral. On earth, atoms always strive for that neutral state. But it can happen that an atom has a positive or a negative charge. This means that it has one or more electrons, too much or too little, so the protons' charge does not match the electrons' charge. An atom becomes an ion if it is thrown out of balance.

 ## How plants communicate via wired networks

Plants have a nervous system too. Electrical signals in plants and animals were first measured and described over 200 years ago. Since then, the flow of new discoveries on action potentials, plant neurobiology and electrical signalling in plants has continued [9*]. Although research into signalling by chemical substances has increased considerably, new generations of researchers have emerged who have continued to focus on the electromagnetic side of plants.

Electrical signalling in plants, both over short and long distances, seems to be increasingly one of the most efficient ways for cell-to-cell communication. Furthermore, the phloem of plants appears to serve as a cable for electricity. Gradually, this phloem is now being considered as a type of green electricity cable that facilitates electrical transmission. That electricity turns out to be generated the moment plants become damaged or 'catch a cold', for example. One of the ways in which the change in power of the electricity could be measured was with the help of aphids that served as bioelectrodes [10*].

Plants each have their own internal wired telephone system. Garden cress leaves and stem vessels serve as electricity cables. In this plant, charges are measured that can move at a speed of 9 cm/s. They send out these electrical signals in order to coordinate their defence, among other things, and in response to changes in light, fluctuations in temperature, and so forth. By connecting the leaves of the garden cress to a few electrodes, researchers discovered that there was no change in electrical potential when cotton leaf worms moved over the leaves. But as soon as the worms began to eat from the leaves, electrical impulses immediately appeared, exactly at the spot on the plant where the worm was having its lunch. The signals spread lightning-fast to the other leaves. Although 9 cm/s seems slow compared to the speed of electrical signals travelling through the mammalian nervous system, which can reach up to 100 m/s, it is comparable to the speed of nerve signal propagation in mussels, for example. The genes involved in transmitting the electrical signal in plants produce channels in a membrane just inside the plant's cell walls; the channels preserve the electric potential by arranging the passage of charged ions. These genes are an evolutionary equivalent to the ion-regulating receptors animals use to transmit sensory signals in their bodies [11*, 12*].

The question is whether this should not radically change our way of looking at plants. For if plants and trees are life forms that think, feel and react with slow electrical impulses like a brain system with nerves, so to speak, could this mean that they register more, perceive more and experience more than we presently assume?

The moment a caterpillar bites a leaf, a glow of fluorescent light flushes over the other leaves so that the whole plant can prepare for future attacks by the caterpillar and its relative species. The fluorescent light follows the calcium pathways while it flashes across the plant's tissue. And if the plant is injured by a caterpillar bite in a particular spot, the rest of the plant activates its defence mechanism. In response to any kind of damage, plants 'light up' and electrical signals flow to all the other leaves. It then takes just a few minutes for the defence-related hormones to also be activated in the more distant leaves. These defence hormones help the plant to prepare itself. The concentration of chemical substances in the plant that are harmful or not tasty to caterpillars increases and the attackers take to their heels, if they have any [13*].

How Peace lilies regulate the balance between positive and negative ions

Ions on earth live a short life. Indoors, they live on average 30 seconds before they come into contact with tiny dust particles, to which they immediately attach themselves, to then instantly fall to the ground. Ions can live a few minutes longer in the open air. The amount of dust there is generally less. Here on earth, ions always strive for a neutral state. Some of them are neutralized immediately after their formation and others last longer, depending on the circumstances. Ions tend to bind to dust particles, which makes them heavier than the surrounding air and causes them to whirl down. Negative ions, for example, also adhere to bacteria in the air and render these harmless by charging them electrically.

A study involving Peace lilies, Strobilanthes and Saint Bernard's lilies, among other things, concluded that plants in general can stabilise the ion concentration indoors and reduce its fluctuations. These plants help to increase the concentration of negative ions and reduce the concentration of positive ions. Optimal ion concentrations could not be achieved by plants alone [14*]. There are all kinds of delicate ion-based circuits between trees, plants and the ecology.

The sensitivity of plants to artificial EMFs

The air near electrical equipment is saturated with positive ions. Also, the life span of negatively charged ions is significantly shorter under the influence of magnetic fields. Most buildings have a lot of electrical equipment nowadays, which cause indoor negative ions to evaporate quickly. It is unknown how the increasing presence of artificial high-frequency EMFs affects the ion-controlled communication systems of humans, animals and plants. This has hardly been researched. Although it is unknown through which mechanisms the electric life of plants can be influenced by artificial EMFs, it is indeed known that this influence takes place.

In the introduction the potato plant was mentioned, and the way a strong magnetic field led to much bigger plants, with bigger potatoes. Everywhere small-scale studies have been conducted into the influence of electric current on plant growth. In one experiment romaine lettuce, or cos lettuce, was exposed to an electric current which made the lettuce grow faster [15*]. That is all very nice and promising. But the most important point in most of these kinds of experiments is missed and this is the fact that plants react to electrical signals and magnetic radiation. There is no overarching theory for the life of plants and animals in an electromagnetic ecosystem, so there is also no idea how to evaluate the consequences of exposure to artificial EMFs. In the latter study, however, it was observed that cos lettuce had difficulty coping when the volume control button of the electricity supply was turned up too far.

Parts of the electric ecosystem such as trees, bushes and flowers are exposed to artificial EMFs on an increasing scale. In order to illustrate the electro-sensitivity of plants, here are a few examples.

I **Duckweed** - The effect of electromagnetic radiation from a transmission mast on the aquatic plant duckweed caused abnormalities in the shape and development of the duckweed after 55 days of radiation. Permanent irradiation of the duckweed, which normally has a life expectancy of 87 days, caused the plants to die after 67 days, on average. The irradiated plants also had fewer offspring [16*].

I **Pine trees** - Pine needles and cones were collected from the tops of old pine trees at four locations near the Skrunda radar station transmission mast in Latvia. The stress in the trees caused by the pulsed high-frequency electromagnetic fields of the Skrunda transmission mast was then measured. Result: the radiation caused accelerated resin production, genetic abnormalities and accelerated ageing of the trees [17*].

I **Tomato plants** - Electromagnetic 0.9 GHz fields cause molecular reactions in tomato plants [18*].

I **Soy** - After two hours exposure to high-frequency radiation from transmission masts, the growth of soybean seedlings decreased [19*].

I Trembling aspen or aspen - In North America, numerous cases of aspen loss have been recorded in the last half-century and a massive mortality of young trees of this species has been observed in Colorado since 2004. Research into this suggests that high-frequency radiation from transmission masts has a strong adverse effect on the growth rate and mortality of trembling aspens [20*].

Other examples of the impact of exposure to artificial EMFs on the natural functioning of plants can be found in the chapter on the consequences for animals and plants.

How far does the electric communication network of plants reach

Plants not only transmit electrical signals and light messages within their own circles, their own plant domain. They are also capable of communicating with other plants over short and long distances and of warning them of imminent danger, for example.

Trees and plants talk to each other secretly by means of electrical signals and jointly use a shielded intranet. We have underestimated the potential of plants. While researchers carefully begin to learn to decipher bits of the language of plants, we get a whole new picture of the green, leafy world of which we are a part. So, plants transmit information through electrical impulses and use a system of voltage-based signalling that is highly reminiscent of the nervous system of animals. It turns out to be surprising what plants can do.

Researchers started mapping the multitude of dynamic electrical signals in broad-leaved plants. One of the things that became apparent was that, by using a special Phytl Signs device, electrical signals of plants can be studied over a long period of time and it is possible to start seeing patterns that are related to reactions to changes in the vicinity. This gives research into the life of plants a spectacular turn. Because then the question becomes: what do plants actually react to - to other plants, to bacteria that transfer plant diseases, to birds, to temperature changes, to attacks by insects, to the cat and perhaps even to a face? Where does it end? More than 20 plant research institutes worldwide are currently involved in research into the electrical interaction of plants with their environment. Decoding electrical signals of plants has begun and promises to be as spectacular as the decoding of the Egyptian hieroglyphs by Champollion [21*].

The trees in the forest are connected via an underground network and work together with useful fungi that form an intricate network of small, threadlike strands between tree roots. One teaspoon of earth contains kilometres of these filaments. The tree produces about 30 percent of the food for the fungi and, in turn, the fungi absorb nutrients for the soil that are available to the tree. Trees exchange chemical, hormonal and slow pulsating electrical signals via an underground network. Messages sent from tree to tree are often distress signals warning of drought, disease or insect attacks. Other trees will change their behaviour or adapt their defences to prepare for the upcoming battle after receiving the messages. Now, even electrical signals are measured and recorded from trees that are being chopped down. The trees send these signals to other trees in the area. It is not yet known what those trees then do with this information [22*].

Flowers advertise by means of electric fields. Their methods of communication are at least as advanced as those of an advertising agency. The chapter on bees describes extensively how pollinators are able to read the electrical signals of flowers the way people read advertisements. But for an advertisement to be successful, it must reach its target group. Researchers have now discovered that flowers also have their equivalent of neon advertisement - patterns of electrical signals that send information to insects. And, as mentioned earlier, plants are usually negatively charged and emit a subtle electric field. Bumblebees, on the other hand, generate a positive charge that can reach up to hundreds of volts as they fly through the air. The potential difference between the insects and the flower ensures that an immediate transfer of information can take place. By inserting electrodes into the stems of petunias, researchers demonstrated that the potential of a flower changes when a bumblebee lands on it and stays there for a few minutes. Bumblebees are also able to detect and distinguish different types of floral electric fields. When these insects are given a learning test, they are faster at learning the difference between two colours when electrical signals are available. Bumblebees and flowers therefore have an electrical relationship [23*].

 ## Plants maintain contact with the earth's magnetic field

Cosmic rays from the sun and other interstellar sources arriving on earth split air molecules as soon as they come into contact with the earth's atmosphere. This is the creative cause of most of the natural ionization on earth. As all cosmic radiation enters through the upper layers of the atmosphere initially, the influence of ionized air molecules is strongest there, hence that level of the atmosphere is called the ionosphere.

Lightning flashes are responsible for most of the largest production of ionized air molecules that reach the lower levels of the atmosphere and are a direct derivative of the intensity with which cosmic rays hit the earth. Lightning flashes are the derivative of solar and interstellar winds that interact with the geomagnetic field and the atmosphere. So, basically, we live directly under the influence of permanent ion rains from the distant and nearby cosmic environment. These rains come down on us in an increasingly intense and powerful way, because the power with which the geosphere protects the planetary ecosystem is steadily decreasing.

The moon also influences the ionization process on earth and, as we have seen in the chapter on higher spheres, plants also influence the moon by sending massive amounts of oxygen to the moon during its seven-day stay in the geosphere's magnetotail.

Plants have the same protein that allows birds to navigate on the energy lines of the earth's magnetic field. Does this also mean that plants register the earth's magnetic field? Studies have been done that indicate they do indeed react to both the strong and weak magnetic fields of the earth. Cryptochrome, the blue-light receptor protein in birds, enables them to detect the earth's magnetic field. Cryptochromes are activated by light, they then become sensitive to a magnetic field. Strangely enough, the same protein has been found in plants, enabling them to react to magnetic fields too [24*].

Some researchers now suggest that changes in force, intensity and polarity of the earth's magnetic field seem to play an important role in all kinds of plant biological processes as well as in their evolutionary process [25*].

The big question is, of course, what applications a plant itself has for these skills? Would plants with these skills regulate their processes in response to variations in the geomagnetic field? How does the magnetic field affect plant development? If all plants and animals tune to the earth's magnetic field, is it unthinkable that these changes in the geomagnetic field also cause all kinds of changes in the electric ecosystem? How many risks do we want to take with the random addition of all kinds of artificial high-frequency radiation fields in a system that naturally works entirely by means of electricity and magnetism?

Electric plant dialect

Trees can produce a voltage ranging from 20 up to hundreds of millivolts. What do trees need these impulses for?

Cos lettuce starts to grow faster after exposure to an electric current

Plants maintain contact with the earth's magnetic field. They have the same protein that allows birds to navigate

Stem vessels of the garden cress serve as electricity cables

Plants phone each other via an underground network of calcium threads

Peace lilies regulate the balance between positive and negative ions

Trees charge the atmosphere. Ion concentrations above forests are twice as high compared to grasslands

Because the eucalyptus tree gives its pollen a negative charge, the pollen starts to float on the negative magnetic field of the earth

Humans

The electromagnetic anatomy of humans

In 1790, Antoine de Lavoisier, the father of modern chemistry, convinced the French academic community that stones can never fall from the sky. Because of his enormous merits in chemistry and his authority as a scientist, no one dared to contradict him. Afraid of being condemned as medieval or unscientific, all museums in Paris and the rest of France immediately threw away their entire collection of meteorites. That is why across France nothing is left of the collection of meteorites found before 1790. If a country is prepared to destroy all indications of the existence of falling rocks, the question is: what other facts and truths have been purged from the collective memory for fear of going against the prevailing views?

Like Linnaeus, Lavoisier was concerned with names, names of elements, and like Linnaeus, life for Lavoisier was a great voyage of discovery. He studied chemistry, botany, astronomy, law and mathematics. The first elements were named. Under the influence of chemistry, new chemical axioms were formed that were very compatible with the growing desire for a more materialistic view of life at the time. A new implicit law came into being, dictating that everything works by chemistry. Thus everyone began to focus on the ordering and reordering of atoms. The discoveries made by Lavoisier and others from that time fed the climate in which realism could emerge. Realism was a 19th-century movement in art, literature and theatre, in which the physical reality was central. It led mankind to look at the world as a materialistic, chemical composition. Any indication that questioned the axiom of reality had to disappear. This is understandable, because the discovery of the new insights needed space. The ultimate truth, however, lies not so much in a single level of perception. And this was also the example set by Lavoisier, Van Leeuwenhoek and Linnaeus - specifically that - the curiosity about the various facets of life made cross-connections and brought perception.

We know very well how electricity behaves *in* wires, but most people have no idea at all of the electromagnetic fields that swirl *around* wires. These fields do not seem to be of any use, so we ignore them. But things that do not seem useful at first glance can certainly have consequences. Because although electricity seems to run safely through a wire in the wall behind the couch to the lamp, we sit quietly on that couch, reading, amid the electromagnetic fields with a diameter of sometimes over two metres which travel along with the electric current through the wire. How much energy do these fields carry? What type of EMFs are in it? Are they always nice, clean 50 Hz fields or can they also change? What kind of influence do all the different frequencies in these fields have on our bodies?

No matter how the facts are arranged, the human body remains first and foremost a conductor of EMFs: for the heart and brain, the nerves and muscles, the blood and pineal gland, the ears and skin, the sperm cells and egg cells, the endocrine system and the human mind.

James Maxwell has made us aware that an electric current cannot exist without a magnetic field. So the various types of electrical activity in the body cannot take place without all kinds of magnetic fields dancing around it, all interacting with each other, as is the case around the power cables in walls. So the human body is much more a radiant electromagnetic field than a bag full of chemicals. Einstein added the following: *"The field is the sole governing agency of the particle."*

Approximately two-thirds of the human body consists of water that contains a lot of salt, metals and minerals. Salt accounts for about 0.4 percent of the body's weight. This is consistent with seawater. A conductor is something that allows the flow of electric charges in one or more directions. Pure water does not conduct electricity. Impurities in water, such as salts and metals, do allow for conduction of electricity. When salts are dissolved in water, they separate into different electrically charged atoms, called ions. So all the nerves, bones and muscles in the human body are conductors of electricity. However, the body is resistant to electric charges. This is because our body is made up of cells. In this context, cells are small packages of salt water, surrounded by membranes made of fats, oils and proteins. Oils are very poor conductors. Thus, although the presence of salt water allows for an electric current in the human body, the membranes act as barriers and offer a natural resistance. What is a resistance? A resistance is something that electricity cannot easily pass through. When electricity is, nevertheless, forced to pass through a resistance, the energy in that electricity is often converted into another form of energy, such as light or heat. One example of this is a light bulb. The reason a light bulb glows is that electricity is forced to pass through a resistance that converts energy into light. Researchers such as Fritz-Albert Popp have discovered that the human body receives, processes and transmits light [1*, 2*].

The electric life of bones

No one is able to function even for one minute of one day without the support of our bones. Bones are remarkably light, offer protection and are super strong. Thanks to his extensive study of the structure of bones, Gustave Eiffel could build the

Eiffel Tower. Because so much attention is always paid to the phenomenal basal characteristics of bones, we may overlook an even more important function. The first interesting discovery is to consider bones as accumulators of various types of energy. The second is to see bones as a beacon of radiation. Bones have a measurable radiation. In this respect, bones are not just there for physical support and protection. They also appear to form an advanced battery system that can store electric charges of various natures and frequencies.

Bones are electromagnetic accumulators and have electrical properties. If pressure is applied to them, for example, they produce an electric current. They can receive, store and release electricity again whenever needed [3*].

This means that a forest walk, going to the gym, taking the stairs instead of the elevator and taking the children to school by bike are all physical exercises that generate electricity in the bones. If a bone breaks, rehabilitation under expert supervision might be shortened by loading them. With almost every movement where the bones are loaded, electricity is generated that can heal bone damage and fractures more quickly. Consequently, bone electricity can be used to promote bone growth in case of fractures [4*].

 ## Electric muscles

Doctors can measure the electrical signals produced by muscles. Electrical muscle stimulation is the induction of muscle contractions by electrical impulses. In recent years this has received increasing attention for several reasons: it can be used in strength training, in rehabilitation and as a test tool for evaluating the muscle function. The impulses are applied to the skin near the muscles using electrodes, often in the form of pads that are glued to the skin. The impulses mimic the action potential coming from the central nervous system, which causes the muscles to contract.

The pulse signals received by the muscles are: (1) low frequencies (1-10Hz) with a long pulse duration that improves the oxygen supply to the muscle. These pulse signals have a restorative and relaxing effect through contractions while stimulating blood circulation in the muscles and disposing of waste products at the same time. (2) Pulse signals with higher frequencies (20-50Hz) which load a muscle in such a way that the muscle structure is particularly improved. (3) Higher frequencies (60-90Hz) can be used to strengthen and increase muscle size.

The signals used by mobile phones also appear to have an impact on muscles. Research on muscle exposure to 0.9 GHz mobile phone EMFs showed that these EMFs had an unexpected effect on the pattern of muscle contractions in animals.

The conclusion drawn from the study was that the findings point to a wide range of adverse non-thermal effects of electromagnetic radiation, particularly on animal muscles [5*]. Is there a fundamental difference between animal muscles and human muscles? If we are training our muscles in the gym, how many people are wearing their mobile phones on their bodies? What are its effects?

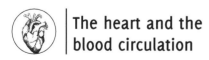 ## The heart and the blood circulation

In 1924 Dutch researcher Willem Einthoven received the Nobel Prize for inventing the string galvanometer for measuring and recording heart activity. This was one of the earliest instruments that could convert the electric currents of the human heart into a kind of cardiac recording. It marked the beginning of the electrocardiogram (ECG). After many centuries of merely physical observations of the heart, the heart suddenly entered the human consciousness as an electrical organ. Strangely enough, Einthoven's original machine was more accurate at recording electrical data about the heart than many of the modern devices that would follow. Moreover, Abramson confirmed only ten years later that blood also carries an electric charge. The idea of the heart and blood circulation as a bioelectric circuit was born [6*]. In 1963, the magnetic field of the human heart was subsequently measured and recorded (MCG).

As research on the heart was further deepened, the heart turned out to actually be a formidable generator of electrical energy, a generator that produces a magnetic field that surrounds the whole human body. This field is like a magnetic sphere in itself. The heart appears to contain many more 'brain cells' than was originally thought. It seems to work with an as-yet undiscovered intelligence. The radiation field of the heart is even 50 times stronger than the field of the brain. The field as measured in an electrocardiogram is about 60 times more powerful than the brain waves recorded in an electroencephalogram (EEG). The heart is the first organ to function during foetal development. As it beats, it emits radiation waves that contain crucial information. So, electrical energy in the body is not only converted into heat, it also has a signal effect that connects everything in the body to everything by means of EMST. These flows of information are received by all cells of the foetus and influence its development. According to neurocardiologists, 60 to 65 percent of heart cells are neuron cells, not muscle cells. The field of the heart can be detected up to more than four metres from the body. The study also shows that the electromagnetic field of heart energy can affect others. A parent holding a baby surrounds the baby with the energy field of the parent's heart [7*]. These early research results deserve support because of their far-reaching consequences. What does it mean that the spheres of influence of one person influence the spheres of influence of another?

The composition of the field around the body is partly generated by the heart and carried by the blood. The blood acts as a kind of hard disk for electromagnetic energy. In a sense, the blood also generates its own electromagnetic body. It flows through the entire system and collects charges everywhere: from the heart, from the liver, from the lungs, from the brain, and so on. This function of the blood as a distributor of electric currents was researched as early as 1941 [8*]. However, this electrical anatomical perspective on the human being repeatedly disappeared from the collective memory, just like Lavoisier's meteorites. Why? What was going on? Why were the electromagnetic fields around the cables in the wall and the electromagnetic fields around the human body not researched in depth anywhere, while physics teaches every student from an early age that these fields exist?

The endocrine system

Hormones and neurons work on the basis of signals, which is also the determining factor for the endocrine system to regulate bodily functions. For that reason, it appears that electrical devices can also have disturbing influences on the endocrine system [9*].

One study showed that the endocrine system is extremely sensitive to the influences of low-frequency EMFs [10*]. A later study evaluated the adverse effects of high-frequency EMFs on the endocrine system of children and young adults.

The immune system

Electromagnetic stimulation of the vagus nerve with specific frequencies works well in the treatment of epilepsy, depression, inflammations, strokes, autoimmune diseases, heart and lung failure, obesity and pain control [11*].

Electrostimulation of the ankles with a 9-volt charge helps to heal an overactive bladder. The ankle nerves cross the bladder nerves at the level of the spine. According to the researchers, hundreds of patients could be helped with this method because it is very easily done at home [12*].

There is no need to give the immune system a helping hand by electrical stimulation of the vagus nerve. The immune system also appears to have its own methods for working with natural EMFs, such as the white blood cells that kill bacteria and fungi by electrocuting them [13*]. Conversely, it is not surprising that artificial EMFs also produce immunity responses. For example, a link has been discovered between artificial EMFs and autoimmune diseases. A study with 64 patients suffering from autoimmune diseases, including rheumatism, showed that after wearing a nightcap woven from fine silver wire to protect the brain against high-frequency EMFs, 90% of the patients experienced improvement of symptoms. The control group wore nightcaps without silver wire [14*].

Charged humans

The immune system utilizes natural electrocution when healing the body. White blood cells use this to kill bacteria and fungi. Electricity can also accelerate wound healing

Wounds produce weak EMFs, and the cells are capable of feeling that electricity and follow its instructions to build new tissue with it

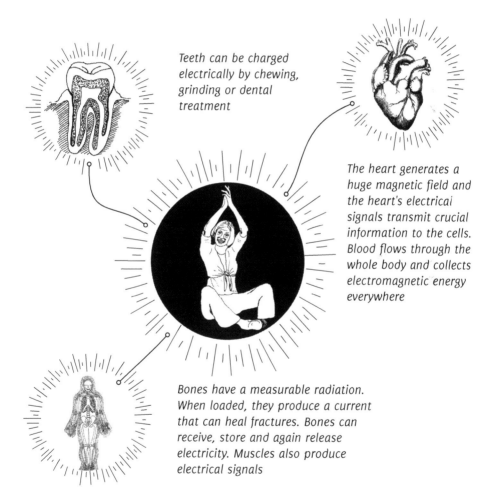

Teeth can be charged electrically by chewing, grinding or dental treatment

The heart generates a huge magnetic field and the heart's electrical signals transmit crucial information to the cells. Blood flows through the whole body and collects electromagnetic energy everywhere

Bones have a measurable radiation. When loaded, they produce a current that can heal fractures. Bones can receive, store and again release electricity. Muscles also produce electrical signals

 The
senses

| Nose and smelling

People can detect at least one trillion different smells. It has long been thought that the human nose could only distinguish about 10,000 smells, but it turns out there are many more [15*].

We do not even have the language to name them all, so how can we ever become aware of them? The worlds in which our nose can smell seem to extend far beyond the horizon of our present consciousness. It would take a whole generation of new Linnaeuses and Lavoisiers to describe and map these unknown aromatic nuances. Thus recently, the myth that humans have the worst nose in the animal kingdom was refuted. Neuroscientists established that the human nose can distinguish odours even better than rats and dogs. The human DNA appears to have no less than about thousand genes for the smell receptors, of which only 390 are active. The cause of this 'smell blindness' seems to be more self-chosen than evolved. The essence of human odour awareness seems to lie in personal development of the ability to process odour information. According to the researchers, this often happens unconsciously and could be developed much more consciously, for example, the way perfumers and vinologists do. So yes, maybe we do not have the language yet, but nothing prevents us from creating new language for aromatic nuances. The idea that our sense of smell is absolutely deplorable compared to the sense of smell animals have, is therefore completely wrong [16*].

Like many animals, humans also appear to have a minuscule crystal, magnetite, which is located in the bone structure between the eyes, just behind the nose. We know from the studies discussed that this crystal connects animals, through EMST, with the earth's magnetic field, in many intuitive and intelligent ways. So why don't we teach people at school to develop these inner techniques? Why do we learn to work with a smartphone in our hands and not with the smartphone in our heads? [17*].

I Eyes and seeing

Approximately 70% of all receptors of the human body are in the eyes. The eyes can recognize 10 million different colours. Light travels at a speed of 300,000,000 metres per second. Light can travel around the earth 7 times in 1 second. The eyes are capable of seeing and working at these incredible speeds, but the question is: can our consciousness cope with what the eyes see? What do we see in the blink of an eye? Millions of shapes, spaces, dimensions, colours, movements, textures, objects and perhaps also... energy, electromagnetic fields, radiation and frequencies? The eyes can see it, but are we also aware of what we see?

The eyes have about 125,000,000 light-sensitive cells. With all these capabilities we can only see change. A frog has eyes that do not move. When the frog sits still, it sees nothing. The frog sees what is moving within his field of vision, such as a crawling insect. Because of the movement, the insect comes within vision of the frog and 'zap', its tongue comes out to capture the insect. Unlike frogs, we humans can see what is not moving. This is because our eyes naturally move about 50 times a second. Eyes have the ability to perceive an incredibly broad flow of impressions. They see at 25,000 million bits per second. But what do they actually see in that blink of an eye? This, too, provides further indications for the notion that unseen is not the same as invisible. With our conscious eyesight we only perceive a tiny part of the electromagnetic spectrum now, while the spectrum itself, in addition to visible light, also consists of radio waves, microwaves, infrared light, ultraviolet light, X-rays, gamma rays, and so on. If we were to lay out the whole electromagnetic spectrum on a street with a length of 100 km, then the part we can see now on that scale, i.e. the seven colours, is only 1 metre long. It is very likely that our eyes are pre-coded to see much more of that electromagnetic spectrum. In other words, the eyes and brain are made to see much more than that which we have prepared our minds for.

Then, in 2011, it became clear that people do indeed see the earth's magnetic field directly with their own eyes. At that time, a light-sensitive protein was localised that helps regulate our daily body rhythms. In addition to the ability to visualize the earth's magnetic field, the protein also behaves as some kind of compass in the eyes. In a previous study, the same researchers discovered how fruit flies and monarch butterflies without the innate ability to see the earth's magnetic field could still develop this ability as soon as their bodies were stimulated to produce the protein. The researchers drew the following conclusion: because the protein is also found in the human eye, there is nothing to prevent people from learning to see an electromagnetic field.

Besides the nose, the eyes also potentially connect us to the earth's magnetic field by means of EMST. These discoveries help to understand old stories about the Polynesian seafarers who travelled thousands of kilometres across the oceans without a compass [18*]. This raises the following questions: where did the alienation from our own faculties start and how do we restore contact? Maybe the evolution of the human is not the linear ascending line we so much like to outline for ourselves. Has there maybe been a hitch somewhere?

Tongue and tasting

The tongue has about 10,000 chemical detectors that can detect the taste of a lollipop by touching just a few of its molecules. This hyper-sensory ability of taste is only used very minimally, even when tasting the best of cooking.

Electric charges can develop by mechanical friction, rubbing or the deformation of a crystalline structure. Chewing, grinding or dental treatment can cause teeth to become charged naturally or artificially with an electric charge. It is unknown to what extent such charges affect taste. That has never been investigated.

There are 32 clusters nerves in the mouth and the fact that electric charges are also involved has recently prompted dentists to be much more careful about the type of materials they use to fill cavities. Dentist Lina Garcia articulates in her newsletter of 5 November 2009 that you probably never compared your teeth to storage batteries, or thought of electric current as a side effect of dental treatments. But when you get ionized metal fillings, a crown or an implant, you also get all the ingredients you need to charge the battery in your mouth. Natural ever-present charge in the mouth plays a role in protecting the oral ecology against bacteria, because some people believe that electric charges are capable of germ-zapping. Others believe that, in the past, teeth were used for detection purposes and that the nerves attached to the 32 teeth would act as a kind of recording mechanism for electric charges in the air or from food.

Ears and hearing

The inner part of our ears contains a battery with electric power: the Endocochlear Potential. When the eardrum vibrates, it generates electrical impulses with a voltage of about 100 millivolts. We have known about this 'ear battery' for over half a century and that it is very important for listening.

According to Alfred Tomatis, the ear is an electric power station. In his view, the ear has other equally important functions besides hearing and filtering and analysing sound. As a power plant, the ear has the task of supplying the brain and thereby our whole body with energy. In this respect, the ear is a generator that converts the stimuli it receives into electro-neurological energy to feed the brain. Especially higher frequencies seem to be responsible for an energy boost. The electromagnetic charge sends messages to our joints, bones and muscles using EMST and provides energy to think, create and move [19*].

Being able to hear sound waves is one thing, but hearing EMFs in the same frequency range is another. In a study, one hundred people who reported that they could hear EMFs and were seriously affected by them were exposed to frequencies ranging from 0 to 5 MHz. Twenty-five people responded to the presence of fields and did not respond to fake fields. These 25 people were then included in a new study, along with 25 volunteers who had no symptoms relating to EMF sensitivity. None of these volunteers responded to the presence or absence of the fields. Sixteen of the EMF sensitives (64%) did respond to it. When the latter group was again exposed to the frequencies to which they were most sensitive in the first phase of the study, they were able to detect the presence of EMFs with 100% certainty. The researchers repeated the test and had the same outcome [20*].

Besides common explanations from brain research and psychology, there may also be other more electromagnetic causes to discover why we sometimes hear or see things that don't seem to be there.

I Skin and feeling

The skin is by far the body's largest sense. It weighs about 3.6 kilograms and is about 2 square metres in size. The skin has all kinds of sensitivities. High-frequency sensitivity areas of the skin, such as the fingertips and tongue, have 10 times more pressure receptors than low-frequency sensitivity areas, such as the back and shoulders. Our physical organs are wrapped in this skin tissue that is divided into several zones.

When we walk on a nylon carpet, the electrostatic charges that build up between the carpet and the skin can be as high as 20,000 or 30,000 volts. Electrodermal activity, also known as skin conductance, is the ability of the human body to continuously cause various electrical phenomena in the skin. Electrodermal activity means that skin resistance can vary, depending on the state of the sweat glands. Sweating is controlled by the sympathetic nervous system and skin conductance is an indication for stress or excitement. When the nervous system gets very excited, the sweat gland activity also increases. This causes electrodermal activity to increase. In this way, skin conductance becomes a measure of emotional and mental reactions.

Electric currents experience less resistance when the surface of the skin becomes sweaty; the salty consistency of the sweat is an excellent conductor. Lie detectors use this function. And as soon as an electric current enters the bloodstream, it encounters virtually no resistance, because blood plasma consists of salt water, iron, copper, and so on. This is why blood can also contain charges and can form an electromagnetic field using these charges.

Traditionally, the skin is only viewed as an absorbing sponge layer filled with water. That image is incorrect, because the twisted portions of the sweat ducts in the epidermis, the outermost layer of the skin, essentially form spiral-shaped antennae that can transmit and receive in the GHz range. The antenna function of the skin depends on the degree of perspiration. That is, it depends on the conductivity of the sweat ducts. There is also a link with stress, both physical and mental and emotional. The presence of sweat ducts leads to a high specific absorption rate of the skin in the extremely high EMF range. This makes us a target for the new artificial high-frequency EMFs through our perspiring skin [21*]. This will be looked at more closely in the next chapter.

A little electricity already accelerates skin wound healing, according to research. Wounds naturally produce weak electric currents, and the cells are capable of feeling that electricity by means of EMST and follow its instructions to build new tissue with it. This phenomenon had already been discovered 150 years ago by German scientist Emil du Bois-Reymond. The knowledge of how our own immune system naturally generates electricity to heal wounds can now be used by scientists to accelerate wound healing processes using additional, artificially generated electric currents. Our body consists of several electric zones. There are differences in charge over the entire surface of the skin. If you compare the charge in the outside world with the electric charge prevailing below the skin, the difference is about 100 millivolts. This is because the skin naturally absorbs positive sodium ions and secretes negative chloride ions, making the area below the skin more positively charged than the area just above it. As long as the skin is intact, the voltage difference remains stable. It does vary a little as a result of stress, emotions and other nervous system activities, but when the skin is injured there is nothing blocking the electric current. Because the electric current then changes from positive to negative, the positive charge flows from the body. The skin is leaking, as it were. As a result, the difference in voltage on the skin at the level of a wound, for example, will be zero volts. But the difference in voltage across the rest of the skin is still 100 millivolts. This voltage difference lasts for hours or even days, until the skin has closed again. It turns out that the difference in voltage provokes various reactions in the healthy skin cells around the wound. It causes cells to divide and move more easily, which promotes healing. The electrical frequencies in the fields also tell the cells where to go, so that they can repair the damaged tissue. If a natural electric charge can help heal wounds, then a more powerful electric charge may help the wound heal more quickly. That is precisely what researchers discovered. They hope that doctors will be able to heal wounds with EMF modulations in the future [22*].

All these references are starting to provide a clear picture of the electrical anatomy of the human body, which is connected to the electromagnetic spectrum in so many different ways: the five types of brainwaves operate at frequencies between 1 and 50 Hz, the eyes see the visible light with frequencies between 400 and 790 THz, hearing can hear frequencies from 20 to 20,000 Hz, and the skin is an antenna for signals in the GHz range. This is likely to be just the tip of the iceberg.

Although it is clear from the above that EMFs have an effect on the human body, so much is still unknown about how EMFs affect cells, organs and systems and what their effects are, both in terms of healing and harming power. We know that EMFs can convert into heat when they come into contact with living tissue. But the way in which the frequencies of natural and artificial EMFs stimulate the body, the cells, the organs and the systems to take action is a fallow field of research.

I Brain and nerves

The brain is made up of 100 billion individual cells that communicate with each other via a complex network of connections. They spend their lives swimming in a pool of salt water, brain fluid, which acts as a conductor. The brain generates enough electricity to light a 20-volt lamp. It uses one fifth of the body's total energy supply. This is amazing, because the brain has no moving parts, which absorb by far the most energy in other parts of the body.

According to Maxwell's law, which states that every electric current produces a magnetic field, the huge number of electrical signals that run through our head, heart and all other systems also produce magnetic fields around the entire body. Scientists began to measure these fields using techniques they called magnetoencephalography (MEG). MEG is a technique that measures the magnetic fields generated by the brain, while the EEG measures the electricity of the brain itself. The distributions of the magnetic fields can be used to analyse information about both the structure and function of the brain [23*].

Electric currents are active in the pineal gland and it appears that the secretion of melatonin by the pineal gland is regulated by those electric currents[24*]. Within the pineal gland electric fields are active that are generated between the earth's surface and the ionosphere. According to research, there is a direct connection between the earth's magnetic field and the pineal gland. The key to this connection appears to be the magnetically charged magnetite particles within the pineal gland [25*].

Another link between the processes of the brain and the earth's magnetic field has been found. Between 1990 and 1997, 2,387 specific notes on dreams were collected. These notes were arranged in five categories. The first category consisted of completely realistic dreams, the middle categories consisted of dreams that gave some but still improbable representations of reality, and the last category consisted of bizarre dreams that had no connection with reality whatsoever. These categories thus reflected their degrees of bizarreness. Daily, the researcher looked up the Kp index for his home town in Perth, Australia, which showed the power of the earth's magnetic activity on site. Using this index and the 2,387 classified notes, a statistically fascinating link became visible between brain processes during sleep and geomagnetic activities under the influence of the sun. As it turned out, the most bizarre dreams occurred on days with the least geomagnetic activity [26*].

The unseen worlds of electricity and magnetism are therefore everywhere in and around the body: the electrical impulses of the heart and the head, the huge electric charges in the cells, the electromagnetic fields that develop around the nervous and blood systems and around the skeleton. But what organises all these spheres of influence? What brings unity of being? These questions lead to a remarkable study by Johnjoe McFadden, who states that the conscious mind is an electromagnetic field. He is convinced that this concept may have far-reaching consequences for our understanding of the mind, free will, the site of our memory and our possible perception of a life after death. The classic picture is that electrical signals are processed in our brains before they are transmitted to the body that reacts to those signals. But where is consciousness located in all those movements of ions, impulses, fields, chemicals and energies? Language, creativity, emotions, logical deduction, our sense of justice and truth are all inconceivable without consciousness. McFadden came to the realisation that every time a nerve sends out a signal, the electrical activity of that signal is also transmitted to the entire electromagnetic field. In contrast to the classical image of solitary electric nerve signals that maintain communication, he proposed a concept in which the electromagnetic field of all processes combined creates a sphere of influence around the head or perhaps around the entire body in which information, signals, choices and impulses are processed, arranged and formed into consciousness. All signals produced in the head and body find their integration in the electromagnetic field of the human. That field establishes connections, makes links and forms consciousness [27*]. That brings us back to Einstein: *"The field is the sole governing agency of the particle."* So, the electromagnetic field of the brain is its consciousness, and the state it is in organizes various energy-bearing parts within that field: feelings, thoughts, emotions, reactions, impulses, preferences, passions. The field provides unity of being.

Possible impact of artificial EMFs on the natural functioning of the human system is described in the chapter on the consequences for humans.

Connected humans

The twisted portions of the sweat ducts in the epidermis essentially are spiral-shaped antennae that can transmit and receive in the GHz range

Electric currents are active in the pineal gland that regulate things such as melatonin production

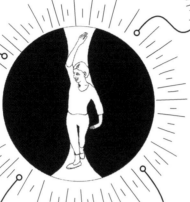

Humans have a minuscule crystal situated just behind their nose, and a light-sensitive protein in their eyes that enables them to smell and see the earth's magnetic field. Dreams are caused by fluctuations in the earth's magnetic field

The brain lives in a pool of salty water that acts like a conductor

The brain generates enough electricity to light a 20-volt lamp

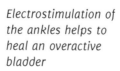

Electromagnetic nervous stimulation can influence epilepsy, depression, inflammations and autoimmune diseases

The human mind turns out to be an electromagnetic field

Electrostimulation of the ankles helps to heal an overactive bladder

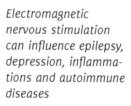

Ears are electric power plants and batteries that provide energy to the brain and body. Especially high frequencies seem to be responsible for an energy boost

Consequences for Animals and Plants

The impact of artificial EMFs on animals and plants

What now follows is a compilation of possible consequences for the electric ecosystem as a result of animal and plant exposure to artificial EMFs. It also provides a brief description of the short-term projections to use artificial EMFs and new transmission techniques as the basis for a wireless world order. The three chapters describing the consequences for animals and plants, for the earth and for humans, have been compiled to fuel dialogue and research on this subject.

The plans with the new artificial EMFs

To be able to live in a world where everything is interconnected, it is important to have many more signals in the air with a much larger frequency range to enable all kinds of things to coexist undisturbed. A kind of thick soup of artificial EMFs is needed, for example, to allow a smart, artificial heart to maintain uninterrupted contact with a monitor in the hospital.

The ingredients of this electric soup will be very different and much more complex in nature than is currently the case. In order to also be able to work with the higher frequency ranges, millions of antennae are projected to be placed near people so that those signals can pass trees, buildings and other objects. Small transmitters will also be installed in homes to make meters smart and have the fridge talk to the supermarket. In addition, an increasing number of satellites will be placed in orbit around the earth to enable the necessary global coverage. The signals will reach us from every possible direction and will be generated from a much wider electromagnetic spectrum.

What this increase in the EMF soup density will do to plants, animals, cells, the immune system and the entire ecosystem in general is unknown and has barely been investigated. So how to start thinking about the consequences? What might a societal dialogue look like that would lead to an informed decision about the future?

2G, 3G, and so on, what is the difference

The nuances of 2G, 3G, and so on, are not the main issue now. By the time we all worry about one of these Gs, another technique with a different name will have been devised. It is important to consider the use of artificial wireless EMFs right in the middle of a world that works by means of natural EMFs. However, to make the story in this chapter tangible, we will also include some information about the Gs here.

The 'G' stands for generation. 1G enabled users to talk to each other wirelessly, 2G allowed for sending messages too, 3G opened the door to mobile wireless internet everywhere and 4G enabled us to do all the above, only much faster. 5G seems to result from this series. It is therefore accepted as the next logical step forward. But 5G does not follow a linear path that was set out by previous generations of wireless communication systems. It is not a logical step forward. The 5G technology is fundamentally different from all the generations we have seen before. It not only accelerates and expands services, but it also completely changes the way mobile transmission is carried out. Not only does it enable us to instantly download and watch videos, it also adds functionalities and wireless strategies we have never witnessed before. Because the results of these new strategies are completely invisible to our eyes, we tend to look away from any possible consequences.

1G   worked at   0,15 - 0,8 GHz - 1980 - 1990
2G   worked at   0,9 - 1,8 GHz - 1990 - 2000
3G   worked at   1,6 - 2,1 GHz - 2000 - 2010
4G   worked at   2 -   8 GHz - 2010 - 2020
5G   will work at   3 - 300 GHz - 2020 - ?

From 1G to 4G constitutes a steady shift to higher operational frequencies. The higher the frequencies, the more energy. With 5G, the increase in operating frequency band is not gradual; it will be exponential. And with the much higher frequencies the wavelength is also shorter - and with the new EMFs, wireless communication is expected to come within the range of frequencies on which cells and human DNA operate. We have already been introduced to bacterial species that multiply under the influence of EMFs from the new range. Milk products that were exposed to radiation at a frequency of 129 GHz were an example of this. In all the product types the acidity decreased, and the number of lactic acid bacteria increased. Some bacteria multiply massively under the influence of high-frequency electromagnetic radiation [1*].

In 2013, a systematic compilation study was conducted of scientific studies published to date regarding potential ecological effects of radio frequency electromagnetic fields (RF-EMF) in the range of 10 MHz to 3.6 GHz. Conclusion - this research shows that in 70% of the studies on the influence of electromagnetic radiation on the natural environment there is a significant effect of GHz-EMFs on birds, insects, bees, plants and other organisms [2*]. There is a huge lack of long-term studies regarding the interaction between GHz-EMFs and plants, animals and the entire ecosystem.

What makes the new technologies so different

The aim of new wireless technologies is to ensure there will be no place on earth without reception and without man-made frequencies and signals. The latest smartphones should work just as well on the North Pole as in New York or Berlin. The new generations of self-driving cars must be able to guide us smoothly through the jungles of Central Africa to Nairobi, Kenya. What are the new technologies that are being employed to achieve that ultimate goal of global coverage as quickly as possible?

First of all, higher frequencies. AM radio signals, for example, are composed of waves that can cover longer distances but have a lower quality than FM signals, but FM signals are limited to city boundaries. Yet they deliver a much better sound quality than AM signals. So, the new generation of transmitter masts will work at frequencies much higher than the ones currently in use. The benefit of a higher frequency is that it can transmit much larger amounts of data at a considerably higher speed. And also, the higher the frequency, the more energy. More energy in the air around us? What does that mean? What if the new generation of radiation sources not only constitutes a linear shift to higher frequencies with more energy, but also crosses an important boundary? What happens if the 10-30 GHz mark exceeds the point at which the radiation frequencies of the radio window stop and something else starts?

People living in nature know that some animals adapt their behaviour when weather conditions change. Ants, for example, seem to be phenomenally accurate predictors of impending changes in weather. The national weather service may forecast with great certainty that the weather will remain sunny and dry, but if ants are starting to make their habitats windproof and waterproof, you can be sure the sun will not shine. Gerhard Ruhensroth-Bauer of the Max-Planck Institute of Biochemistry in Munich explained this mystery by pointing out that ants are extremely sensitive to EMFs from the electromagnetic spectrum radio range. Changing weather types are accompanied by electromagnetic phenomena. Ants sense the frequencies of these phenomena coming from enormous distances [3*].

Meteorological ants

There is a study about all kinds of phenomena that go hand in hand with the use of radio window frequencies, but virtually nothing is known about the frequencies above them.

Because frequencies in the GHz range cannot pass very well through buildings or other obstacles and are also absorbed by plants and rain, new techniques will operate with a very different signal distribution system. The new signals will only be able to cover a distance of about 300 metres. So, the infrastructure needed to apply this technology requires a lot of extra transmitter masts to be placed close together and close to homes, schools, hospitals and offices. Furthermore, satellites will be placed in orbit around the earth to provide the new networks with sufficient density and coverage to enable 'the internet of things'. Because that is the aim: global coverage. The safety argument used here is that because the new EMFs operate at lower intensities the impact on organic matter is lower. But what if it is precisely the other way round? What if signals with a lower intensity are the language cells use to communicate with each other, as we have seen in the chapter on cells? What if it is precisely the frequencies with high intensities that are ignored by cells? What if the new frequencies with whisper-quiet intensities are the signals that cells do listen to, because they themselves communicate with each other in those frequencies, too?

Self-driving cars are currently the most eye-catching example of the many possibilities the new technology will make feasible. These cars have a response ratio of just 1 millisecond, while the human response ratio is about 200 to 300 milliseconds. This means the new technology is much faster than the measurable human ability to respond to complex traffic situations. This automatic reactivity of self-driving cars is made possible by using satellite connections combined with the planned network of transmitter masts along every road and every street. The risk of car accidents and long traffic jams is expected to reduce. All cars will continuously send signals to and receive signals from each other. They will know each other's exact location on the road at all times. They can know this because of another significant difference between the old and new generation in artificial EMF transmission, i.e. MIMO, or multiple-input multiple-output. With MIMO, mobile phones or smart cars contain several antennae that can communicate simultaneously with several devices and enable multiple data streams. In other words, the signal is able to control several devices all at the same time, such as mobile phones, televisions, cars and drones, which receive signals by the same transmission node, in the same area, without losing strength. In short, the new wireless transmissions are nothing like the current mobile technology. MIMO will create a dense electro-soup with frequencies humans have never been exposed to before. Until now, safety limits have been based on experiments with radiation coming from one device or mast that transmits in one direction. What will happen to all organic life if the radiation comes from all directions at once, including from the air by satellites? If we are not even convinced of the health risks resulting from the radiation from one single mobile phone or transmitter mast, what could be the health risks associated with a new much thicker electric soup that will be poured over the entire ecosystem without any guarantees about its safety? No matter how exciting and easy and profitable the new world with its much higher EMFs promises to be, the question is whether these supposed benefits will outweigh the health price we ourselves, but also the animals and plants, will possibly have to pay.

Because of the increase in the huge amounts of MIMO radiation and frequencies, there is a danger that all kinds of electrical disturbances will occur, with all the consequences this entails. With MIMO, this interference within the electro-soup has the potential to get completely out of hand. To prevent this, another technology has been developed, namely beam formation. Because of much higher frequencies, the new GHz-EMFs will have a much greater capacity to concentrate in the form of beams. This means that signals can be bundled and targeted specifically at areas where more data traffic is required. The technique of beam formation allows the new EMFs to be deployed as a weapon, should they fall into the wrong hands. So, the new antennae can be oriented and focused, whereas until now they have only had the ability to radiate in all directions. It is the difference between a lamp that shines its light in all directions and a laser that bundles all that light into a single beam.

At the moment, wireless signalling is controlled by signals that travel back and forth at the same frequency. But with full duplex, devices can simultaneously transmit and receive instead of having to wait until the transmission is complete before they can receive. It is safe to say that with all these new techniques the air above our heads and around us will become packed with activity. It is also interesting to note that no democratic debate has taken place on the introduction of these technologies as yet.

A few examples of consequences for animals and plants

| Monkeys - The behaviour of monkeys changes significantly by exposing them to the new, much higher 5.62 GHz EMFs [4].

| Bees - Exposure of bees to electromagnetic radiation fields from pylons (50 Hz) has all kinds of biological effects [5]. Experiments and research have indeed shown that these strong omnipresent fields cause disturbance in the communication between bees, that their sense of direction and sense of orientation, which is tuned to the earth's magnetic field, is disrupted and that some bees become so aggressive that they start stinging each other to death. Other bees leave their hives [6,7,8]. The development of young bees is also adversely affected [9]. In yet another study, bees were exposed to 50 Hz high-voltage fields, after which their wings, antennae and body hairs began to vibrate intensely. Their behaviour changed and it also became evident that the fields caused them painful shocks [10,11]. Other references on bees from the last 14 years: 12* - 23*.

| Bacteria - Bacteria are killed by irradiating food and vegetables with EMFs. Washing fruit and vegetables after having removed them from their plastic bags could therefore be a thing of the past. According to research, microbes such as salmonella can be killed with a short electric shock in just a few seconds now. This treatment will not only kill bacteria, but also deactivate viruses and fungal spores that are still present on the food inside the packaging [24*].

| Trees - A study aimed to investigate whether there was a link between tree damage and exposure to high-frequency signals from transmitter masts. A detailed long-term field monitoring (2006-2015) was carried out in the cities of Bamberg and Hallstadt, Germany. During monitoring, observations and photographic images of unusual or unexplained damage to the trees were made, as well as measurements of electromagnetic radiation. The measurements of the trees revealed significant differences between the damaged side of the tree facing a transmitter mast and the other side not facing the mast. A tree control group in low-emission areas without any visual contact to a transmitter mast showed no damage. Statistical analysis demonstrated that electromagnetic radiation from transmitter masts is harmful to trees. These results are consistent with the fact that damage to trees from mobile phone masts usually starts on one side and extends over the whole tree over time [25*]. Because trees seem so badly affected by radiation from masts, Helmut Breunig compiled an extensive observation guide about them [26*].

| Yeast - Yeast cultures were exposed to 42 GHz. Weak GHz irradiation of aqueous yeast cultures was found to affect the growth rate of that yeast in a frequency-selective manner. Depending on the frequency, which was nearly 42 GHz, both increases and decreases in growth rate were observed. The resonance bandwidths are in the order of 0.01 GHz. Simple thermal effects could be excluded. One year later, the study was repeated with the same results [27*, 28*].

I **Shark, ray, tuna, salmon, mackerel, trout** - In the world, for almost a century now, electromagnetic fields have been introduced in oceans, bays, estuaries and seas to connect offshore drilling rigs and wind farms to the mainland. Despite this, very little is known about the consequences for the underwater environment due to the application of EMFs. In 2011 an overview was made available concerning the many different effects on sharks, rays, tuna and various salmon, trout and mackerel species. This overview reports on disturbances in migration patterns, navigation problems, behavioural abnormalities and all kinds of other effects on fish [29*].

I **House sparrows 1** - A clear decline in the population of house sparrows has been observed in the United Kingdom and in several Western European countries in recent decades. A study examined whether this was also the case in Spain and whether electromagnetic signals from transmitter masts were related to the decline in the sparrow population. Measurements were taken at 30 points during 40 visits to Valladolid in Spain between October 2002 and May 2006. The results of this study support the hypothesis that the presence of transmitter masts is indeed related to the observed decline in the sparrow population. According to this study, the apparent strong dependence between bird density and radiation could be used for a more extensive study [30*].

House sparrows 2 - In another study, the effect of long-term exposure to electromagnetic radiation from mobile phone base stations (GSM) on house sparrows during the breeding season was studied in six residential areas in Belgium. The results of the study show that fewer house sparrow males were spotted on locations with high radiation from GSM base stations. These results support the idea that long-term exposure to higher radiation levels negatively affects the presence and behaviour of house sparrows in the vicinity of GSM masts [31*].

Dogs - A dog kennel in Allegan County, United States, lost more than 120 litters of Shetland sheepdogs in 12 years. Many of the puppies that died were deformed. But also many of the puppies that survived were deformed. Similar effects were seen in Persian cats, German Shepherds and Golden Retrievers. The problems started after the drilling of a deeper well and the building of a new concrete/metal kennel in 1969. Before that time, the owner of the kennel had successfully bred and raised 15 litters of sheepdogs in an old wooden chicken shed. Due to health problems, the kennel's owner did not breed any more dogs until the end of the eighties but resumed work in 1989, initially with some success. However, in 1992, the reproductive problems came back. Two dairy farmers in Allegan County, who had similar health and reproductive problems in cows, were involved in the study. Tests were carried out and revealed that stray voltage was present in all cases. Using various measuring instruments, the presence of stray currents in the dog kennel and with the dairy farmers was found to be the cause of the problems [32*].

Stray voltages prove to be dangerous to dogs, cats and cows

I Cows - In one experiment, cows were kept close to a TV and mobile phone mast. Cows that began to exhibit abnormal behaviour were moved 20 kms away, at great distance from the transmitter mast. Within 5 days the animals behaved normally again. When the cows were brought back to the location close to the transmitter mast, their abnormal behaviour returned [33*].

I Quail eggs - Japanese quail eggs were subjected to 2.45 GHz radiation during the first 12 days of embryo formation. After hatching, the exposed embryos, as well as the unexposed control group, were raised to an age of 22 weeks. The data demonstrate that the exposure of Japanese quails during the time inside the egg reduced the immune potential, among other things [34*].

I Maize and wheat - Various germination experiments where seeds were exposed to a static magnetic field showed that the germination speed of the seeds increased. The plants also grew longer and heavier. In a study conducted under a power line with a variable magnetic field, the effect on wheat and maize cultures was evaluated. The results indicated a 7% reduction in wheat field production underneath the high-voltage cables during the 5-year study. Under the influence of a static magnetic field, the growth and development of plants is often stimulated, while under a variable magnetic field the growth and development of plants is, in fact, inhibited [35*]. Exposure to radiation from pylons has various biological effects in maize. There are all kinds of physiological risks for plants that grow near high-voltage lines. Conversely, the cultivation of plants underneath low-grade electromagnetic fields may improve crops and could be part of future innovations in agricultural techniques [36*].

| **Monarch butterflies** - High-frequency radiation from transmitter masts is threatening the survival of monarch butterflies, garden warblers and robins [37*].

| **Plants 1** - This study analysed 45 scientific publications (1996-2016) describing 169 experimental observations to detect the physiological and morphological changes in plants as a result of non-thermal EMF effects of radiation from mobile phones. 29 species of plants were assessed in this study. Result: 89% of the studies show physiological and/or morphological effects due to exposure of plants to high-frequency radiation. Moreover, the results of these reported studies show that maize, roselle, pea, fenugreek, duckweed, tomato, onion and mung bean prove to be very sensitive to this radiation [38*].

| **Plants 2** - Greek research into the effects of EMFs on plants, birds and trees shows that radiation from transmitter masts affects plant germination and reduces crop yields. Greece has a huge diversity of wild plants with some 6,000 varieties of wildflowers. It can take a long time before it is even noticed on a sufficiently large scale that small plants and flowers are dying. Many are seen as weeds and small plants are difficult to count. Few people notice them [39*].

I Thornback ray - Exposure of the thornback ray to 5 Hz electric fields resulted in disturbances in heart rhythm and respiratory problems [40*].

I Wheat plants - Effects on wheat plants from high-voltage cables (50 Hz) stretching across an open agricultural field were measured. The study's conclusion is that growing wheat plants under high-voltage cables significantly reduces the yield of the plant and that the electromagnetic fields emitted from the cables can be considered to be polluting influences [41*].

I Fish - Electromagnetic susceptibility of fish is varying greatly between species. Sharks and rays appear to be extremely sensitive to alternating-current electric fields with low frequencies up to 8 Hz. Salmonids are slightly less sensitive to the same fields. Eels are particularly sensitive to magnetic fields in the order of a few µTesla [42*].

I Birds - Transmitter masts seem to be deadly to birds, as reports by the American Bird Conservancy say. The 47 different studies that were analysed show that some 180,000 birds from 230 different species died from radiation from transmitter masts [43*].

I Clouds, rain, snow and ice - The head of The National Oceanic and Atmospheric Administration (NOAA) warned the US government on 20 May 2019 not to make too many frequencies available for 5G. NOAA is the American National Weather Service. The problem lies mainly with the 24 GHz frequency. Water vapour, such as a cloud, emits a weak measurable 23.8 GHz signal into the atmosphere. Meteorologists now follow clouds using that frequency, but those measurements will soon no longer be reliable. In practice, this would mean that hurricanes, as an example, would be discovered two to three days later than currently. It would also be much more difficult to predict the path taken by a hurricane when it comes ashore, which could mean the difference between life and death. Nevertheless, the American telecommunications agency FCC has been auctioning the 24 GHz frequency since March 2019. The 24 GHz band is not the only frequency causing problems. Meteorologists also warn about the 36-37 GHz bands used to detect snow, the 50.2-50.4 GHz frequencies used to measure atmospheric pressure and the 80-90 GHz band used to trace ice [44*]. In the Netherlands, the auction of 5G frequencies will start towards the end of 2020.

Animals, Plants and Radiation

Artificial EMFs can destroy microbes such as salmonella. 42 GHz EMFs influence the growth rate of yeast cultures. The immune potential of quails reduces by exposing quails' eggs to artificial 2.45 GHz radiation. 180,000 birds from 230 different species were killed by radiation from transmitter masts

A cloud emits a 24 GHz signal to the atmosphere

Snow can be detected in the frequency range around 37 GHz

Tomatoes, onions and mung beans are sensitive to high-frequency radiation

The behaviour of monkeys changes by exposure to 5.62 GHz EMFs

Radiation from transmitter masts affects cow behaviour, limits the size of sparrow populations, damages trees, limits plant germination, reduces crop yields and threatens the survival of monarch butterflies

Consequences for the Earth

We have seen what bees, frogs, sperm whales, nightingales and sea turtles do with their geomagnetic connections. We have seen how some animals connect to the geomagnetic field via their beaks or via magnetite crystals in their bodies, while other animals, such as chickens, can simply see the magnetic fields of the earth. In addition, we have been introduced to the way bacterial species are so closely entangled with the geomagnetic field that they actually seem to be an extension of it. The question arising from these observations is: what are the consequences of the artificial generation of EMFs for the connection of life to the geosphere? Might they upset natural connections, as we have seen with some migratory birds that become disoriented above cities? There are also questions relating to the new higher frequency EMFs, EMFs that will be activated below the natural filter system of the planet. What impact might the higher frequencies have upon the natural electromagnetic signalling processes that take place in all life on earth? What effects will these high frequencies have, especially if they are chopped into pieces to be transmitted as pulse frequencies? In other words, what are the consequences of global coverage with respect to the internet of things for the earth's entire natural electric ecosystem?

The frequency window of the earth

The earth's filter system makes exceptions for two frequencies, two permanently open windows for specific frequencies from space. In the lower frequency range, this is the radio frequency window. In the higher frequency range, this is the optical window. The existence of these two windows is quite easy to see. A large assembly of radio frequency telescopes is located in Westerbork, the Netherlands. Because radiofrequency radiation from the universe can reach the earth's surface virtually unobstructed, even penetrating the clouds, Westerbork has 14 immense parabolic dish antennae directed towards space. Signals from space enter that window and are listened to 24/7. All over the world, artificial radio transmitters are banned in the vicinity of such radio frequency telescopes, because mobile phones, transmitter masts and Wi-Fi interfere with the detection of radio frequencies from the universe. The other window, the optical window, including parts of the infrared range, is also very easy to see. The sun's light and the sun's heat radiation can reach the surface of the earth unobstructed, otherwise we would not be able to see anything and feel its warmth.

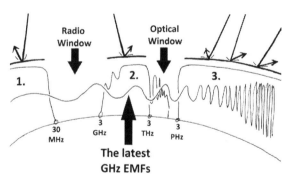

Frequency windows

The earth's electromagnetic filters remain specifically closed for the entire range of frequencies coming from space in the frequency ranges of 1, 2 and 3 in the figure. As of 2020, new EMFs are likely to start the artificial transmission of frequencies in the

GHz range - area 2 in the drawing - through thousands of satellites and millions of transmitter masts. The big question is: why does the earth's geomagnetic field naturally block all the frequencies in area 2? What will happen when new artificial EMFs begin to introduce the very signals that the earth's geomagnetic field blocks? Until now, frequencies from the radio window up to 3 GHz have been used to enable wireless communication. In the meantime, a catalogue of scientific literature has been produced on this subject, which also indicates that these artificial frequencies have adverse effects. With the latest wireless ambitions, we are leaving familiar territory.

We saw that insects best absorb electromagnetic frequencies over 6 GHz and that exposure of insects to such frequencies causes changes in behaviour as well as changes in physiology and morphology [1]. We have also seen how exposure to EMFs in the GHz range can change transport across cellular membranes, alter the activity in cell membranes, and that those EMFs can interfere with DNA, can influence the cell cycle and cause genetic instability [2].

How, in a world full of artificial signals, will natural communication still be possible among bacteria, bees, plants, fish and birds? As discussed in the chapter on humans, the skin is only viewed as an absorbing sponge layer filled with water. That is not the whole picture because the twisted portion of the sweat ducts in the epidermis is in essence a spiral-shaped antenna that can transmit and receive in the GHz range. The antenna function of the human skin in the GHz range depends on the intensity of perspiration, i.e. it depends on the conductibility of the sweat ducts. There is also a link with stress: physical, mental and emotional. The presence of sweat ducts leads to high skin absorption in extremely high frequency bands [3].

Frequencies of the earth's background radiation

In addition to the direct health risks of the increasing electro-soup in the living environment of humans, animals and plants, another risk emerges related to satellites. Putting satellites into orbit around the earth to create global coverage may endanger electromagnetic dynamics that exist high above our heads in the earth's magnetic field, with which the entire electric ecosystem is connected.

The cavity between the D layer of the ionosphere (see figure on page 176) and the earth's surface seems to behave like a large electrical circuit. On average, there are around 2,000 thunderstorms active on earth at any given time. Together they produce about 50 lightning flashes per second. Each lightning burst creates electromagnetic waves that constitute background radiation in the cavity around the earth. The electromagnetic waves are trapped between the earth's surface and the lower part of the D layer. All these electromagnetic waves together combine again and again into a kind of atmospheric heartbeat known as the Schumann resonance. The average frequency of this background radiation is 7.8 Hertz. This frequency remains fairly constant as long as the properties of the earth's electromagnetic cavity remain unchanged [4*]. What is the natural function of this background radiation? What influence does it exert on all life? Some researchers point out that the planet's average background radiation is at present already rising from 7.8 Hz to 11 Hz. Whether the cause is to be found in natural sources, such as the geomagnetic field, which is losing power at an ever-increasing rate, or whether the cause is rather to be found in the artificial transmissions of human origin, is unknown. It is known, however, that the increase in background frequencies varies from one geographical region to another.

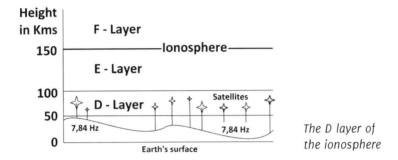

The D layer of
the ionosphere

The many satellites that will radiate their as-yet-unknown frequencies from the ionospheric D layer towards earth might interact with the natural background radiations of the earth. In addition to the connection that all kinds of animals seem to maintain with the geomagnetic field, the ecosystem also seems to tune itself to these natural background radiations. Whales and dolphins, for example, appear to emit signals at frequencies around 8 Hz, which is more or less identical to the frequencies of the background radiation.

The ionosphere has several layers consisting of electrons and electrically charged atoms and molecules surrounding the earth. It stretches from an altitude of about 50 to 1,000 kilometres. The most relevant layer in terms of the new EMFs is the D layer, the inner layer at about 60 to 90 kilometres above the earth's surface. Between the earth and the D layer the natural background resonance is created in which all life takes place and to which all life seems to be attuned.

During space travel it became clear that the 7-8 Hz base frequency is a necessary supplement for the human body. Astronauts who had been in space appeared tired and disoriented upon their return and had to spend weeks in quarantine because their immune system was compromised. Thanks to the generation of a 7-8 Hz artificial electromagnetic field, astronauts can now stay in space shuttles and space stations without too much difficulty.

The natural background radiation helps to synchronize the human biological system with the earth's daily rhythmic cycles. This is how the background radiation synchronizes melatonin production. Melatonin secretion by the body reduces when the frequency of the background radiation becomes disturbed, according to research by Neil Cherry [5*].

Proceeding with a whole global immersion of the entire electric ecosystem in brand-new radiation frequencies without extensively evaluating the risks first, does not seem wise.

The risk is that the new EMFs may also lead to disturbances in the earth's primary background frequencies. What happens if the natural planetary background radiation of 7 to 8 Hz is bombarded with increasingly higher artificial frequency sources? What happens if thousands of satellites start transmitting with the new 3 to 300 GHz radiation regimes, or with pulsed variants in the much lower frequency range? It is unknown what the consequences will be if harmonics of the natural background frequencies become part of the world-wide menu of frequencies. The picture that emerges from the data that led to this book shows in any case that almost all life is closely linked to the earth's electromagnetic processes. Many birds, fish and land animals communicate with and navigate on that earth's magnetic field. And the proposed transmission of GHz frequencies from new satellites in the D layer will probably cause unknown physical, biological, mental or emotional effects. Or nothing at all. Or nothing for years and then suddenly something. As mentioned before, no long and independent research has been conducted into the impact of new GHz EMFs on biological materials. Also, as far as is known, no research has been done into the impact of those EMFs on the natural planetary background radiation.

Consequences for Humans | *The impact of artificial EMFs on humans*

In underpinning the argument that everything in the ecosystem works by means of natural EMFs, it is worth considering the possible consequences for humans, too. What will the body's cells do when new signals with higher frequencies come into view? Will we notice when our cells notice? Will we be able to detect when the artificial signals are changing organic matter? Will that impact be sudden or will it manifest itself so gradually that no one notices? Is it conceivable that the consequences of the impact gain ground beneath the surface of collective consciousness, as was the case with tobacco and asbestos?

With the implementation of all kinds of wireless forms of communication the body no longer has been processing a single frequency, but has been dealing with thousands of other frequencies. Possibly each of these frequencies requires a separate immune system response. This means a cocktail of electro-toxins for the body. This cocktail of frequencies can make people ill. Where do those signals get into our human systems?

Why positive and negative datasets complement each other

Although there are at least as many research results showing that artificial EMFs can cause damage to the ecosystem as there are research results showing that artificial EMFs are harmless, these two datasets do not cancel each other out. On the contrary. Both datasets are vital in the process of gaining a better understanding of how the entire ecosystem works through electricity and magnetism.

We have seen how lactic acid bacteria will grow fast due to exposure to the EMF of specifically 129 GHz. If more research were done into the effect of exposure of these bacteria to frequencies ranging from 0 to 128 GHz and from 130 to 300 GHz, which would show that all these frequencies have no effect at all, these results would not cancel each other out but rather complement each other. They reveal, after all, the frequency-specific reactivity of lactic acid bacteria.

Consequences

Below is a brief collection of research results relating to the potential impact of artificial EMFs on humans. They may provide a platform for evaluation of the potential problems, and may give rise to further research and also encourage dialogue.

I Heart and blood vessels - Red blood cells were exposed to 18 GHz EMFs. This increases the uptake of nanospheres in these blood cells [1*]. What other impact do artificial EMFs have on blood circulation and heart? The following studies emphasize the link between heart palpitations, blood pressure disorders, leukaemia and artificial EMFs. See references: 2* – 11*.

I Head and nervous system - High-frequency artificial EMFs reduce melatonin secretion in animals and humans. Melatonin regulates the circadian rhythm in mammals and is a powerful antioxidant. The production of melatonin by the pineal gland increases at night and melatonin is then spread through the body. It removes free radicals from cells to protect the DNA. Melatonin also has many other functions. It supports the immune system and regulates sleep. Melatonin reduction has many serious biological effects on mammals, including chronic fatigue, sleep disturbances and DNA damage. Melatonin reduction is also associated with arthritis, depression and Alzheimer's disease. Also, there appears to be a link with brain tumours and tinnitus. See references: 1* – 9*.

Ι Immune system - Artificial EMFs appear to disrupt immune functions by stimulating various allergic and inflammatory reactions, as well as having negative effects on tissue repair processes. See references: 1* – 7*.

Ι Bone system - What is the effect of artificial EMFs on the growth and development of the bone structure? Reference: The mineral density of the bone structure of electricians is significantly lower than that of people in the control group 1*.

Ι Mind, emotions and mental state - If the human mind can essentially be defined as an electromagnetic phenomenon, what then is the impact of artificial EMFs on the psychology, the mood and the overall emotional and mental state of the human? Is there a link with for example amnesia, sleep disorders, fatigue, dizziness, loss of concentration, tension, irritation, headaches, learning achievements, stress, depression, and so on? See references: 1* – 16*.

Ι Sperm cells and egg cells - Electricity and magnetism seem to cause differences in behaviour in sperm cells and egg cells. What is the impact of artificial EMFs on the reproductive organs and fertility? See references: 1* – 8*.

Ι Derailment of cell growth - Can artificial EMFs induce healthy human cells to behave unnatural? See references: 1* – 16*.

| Autism - About the possible link between artificial EMFs and autism [1*].

| Metal bed springs - A 2010 study showed that metal bed bases and spring mattresses may be an antenna for EMFs. Metal bed frames and metal springs in mattresses can act as conductors for low-frequency fields and for high-frequency EMFs. According to the researchers, the power of the field sometimes extends up to 75 centimetres above the mattress [1*].

Future

The future no
one expects

The United States' Founding Fathers were inspired by the constitution of the Iroquois in formulating the U.S. constitution. The Iroquois, a federation of several Indian tribes, were the original inhabitants of the northern region of the state of New York. One of the principles of their constitution was 'the 7th-generation sustainability'. Thus the Iroquois' council of wise men committed themselves, when making important decisions, to always consider the impact on 7 generations in the future. However, the Founding Fathers did not integrate this in the U.S. constitution.

What would it have meant for the development of world culture, global economy and technology if they had included this Iroquois attitude of fundamental future orientation in the U.S. constitution? What would it mean for our way of life if all countries were to include this future orientation in their constitutions now?

In the park in front of the cultural centre of the city of Hasselt, in the Belgian province of Limburg, stands a 3D representation of the Iroquois principle. It has a row of six metal silhouettes; the work of sculptor Frederick Franck. The sign says: 'Seven Generations', and has the following text: 'In all our deliberations we must be aware of the consequences of our decisions for the next 7 generations' (the Federation of 6 Nations Iroquois). The first concepts of the 7th generation principle dates from a period somewhere between 1100 and 1500 AD.

If you decide something, then weigh the consequences mindful of the 7 generations to come

What will the life of the seventh generation after us be like? What quality of life will we offer them by virtue of our actions today? Will it be a world where people can look each other in the eye without fear? Will it be a world of compassion, respect, trust and peace? Will it be a world with enough food, clean water and clean air? Will it be a healthy world with an intact electric ecosystem?

Every generation that lives now has just one 7th generation in the future to take care of. If a generation spans about 15 to 25 years, many people will see 3 or 4 generations being born and growing up in their lives. Seven generations are then double this amount. My father reached the age of 92 and became a great-grandfather. He saw the 4th generation; he saw the first contours of the consequences of the actions of his generation.

Will we burden our 7th generation by the decisions being made now, in this day and age, or will we protect them from harm by these decisions? What will their fate be as a result of what we determine, set in motion and allow now? What are the future tragedies that can be prevented now? The tribal elders of the Iroquois Confederacy will have possibly asked themselves questions of this kind.

The 7th generation of rabbits

For animals, the 7th generation comes much sooner than for humans. Rabbits are a good example of this. Three months after their birth, young rabbits can become pregnant themselves. Their gestation period is about one month. So, for them, a new generation can start after four months. In an average human life of 70 years we have outlived 210 generations of rabbits.

Within 3 years there will be a 7th generation of rabbits

In the previous chapters all kinds of natural electromagnetic features of animals have been discussed. In the introduction the idea was proposed that this research project could be written and experienced on 7 levels, in which case this book would be a first beginning of level 1. A characteristic feature of level 1 is that it can go on *ad infinitum*, but also that the quality of the research presented is compiled mindful of the 7th level. Moreover, all levels above it are built on the quality of that 1st level. So, this 1st level is essential.

The spirit of the 7th generation principle applies to all aspects of the ecosystem, such as bears, eucalyptus trees, cow parsley, dogs, kangaroos, frogs, hummingbirds, ants, clouds, rabbits, viruses and so on. This opens the research in all directions, which is also necessary because every animal, and every plant, and every microbe has its own specific electromagnetic aspects, its own connections to the earth's magnetic field. Not evaluating these aspects comes with a price. The human race is about to take decisions that may have far-reaching consequences for the natural ecosystem. In order to emphasize the responsibility for the 7th generation, for example the 7th generation of rabbits which will have seen the light of day within 3 years, here is a selection of existing research results about rabbits. It shows that they are affected frequency-specific by electricity and magnetism in a variety of ways.

The impact of EMFs on rabbits, studied between 1979 and 2016, only relates to a very small frequency bandwidth. It concerns the frequencies between 0.8 and 2.45 GHz. These are the most common frequencies throughout the period of the rise of the mobile phone. The influence of new bandwidths on rabbits has not been studied as yet. Following here is a selection of what is known so far about the sensitivities of rabbits to EMFs.

A group of male rabbits were exposed to a mobile phone radiation frequency of 0.8 GHz, for 14 weeks none stop, and this had a significant impact on the sperm count of these animals [1]. When they experienced continuous radiation of 0.9 and 1.8 GHz frequencies, their breathing was affected [2]. Daily irradiation of rabbits with 1.5 GHz EMFs led to anxiety and alarm responses [3], and exposure of young rabbits to 1.8 GHz radiation caused DNA damage [4]. Radiation frequencies of about 2.4 GHz caused, among other things, changes in their brain activity [5], while radiation of 2.45 GHz caused, among other things, inflammation and lens changes in rabbit eyes [6]. Furthermore, exposure to 2.45 GHz Wi-Fi signals had a direct impact on the heart rate and blood pressure of albino rabbits [7].

The reason why rabbits are so very sensitive to all kinds of radiation frequencies is probably due to their various electrical abilities, such as electroreception, which was discovered in 2003 [8*]. Research, conducted in 2015, has shown that 2.1 GHz radiation can have a positive influence on jaw fracture healing in rabbits [9*]. This last research result opens up a world in which some specific frequencies, which seemed harmful up to that point, can also bring about many more constructive effects.

The natural context for animals and plants is the geosphere. It seems essential to understand the electric ecosystem much better in order to keep it safe, clean and natural, so that the many generations of animals and plants to come can continue to find their future in it. However, as the chapter on higher spheres has already opened up, it seems crucial for people to consider another aspect for the future in addition to preserving the natural ecosystem for the generations to come.

In previous chapters, we have seen that there are indications to assume that much, if not everything, in the ecosystem works by electricity and magnetism, that the smallest possible, the cells, the bacteria and the insects work with it and that the largest possible, the geosphere, the heliosphere and the galactosphere also work with it. The facts have been thoroughly evaluated with studies and examples, and we can conclude that humans, animals and plants work by means of EMFs, that the entire ecosystem is electrically connected to the geomagnetic internet and that we, humans, can also be influenced by higher spheres in terms of our dreams, our state and our temper.

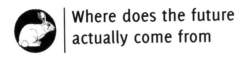# Where does the future actually come from

Will the future only come from technical innovations? And if so, what kind of future vision will technical innovations produce? A world that is fully connected and linked up, the new and smart internet of things, a world full of new sensational techniques? A world with self-driving cars cruising silently through smart cities on their way to smart homes, a world where drones deliver groceries to homes and homes work with artificially intelligent, robot-controlled systems, equipped with virtual reality and all sorts of other useful technological gadgets. It is a sensational world in which all people get the chance to be connected to all the exciting and colourful techniques that wireless network will bring us. It is a vision of a world full of physical convenience, greater efficiency, and distraction for the mind in which loneliness, resistance, degrading work and boredom may have been eradicated. But will it also be a world in which we accept ourselves, the way we currently are, with all our faults and imperfections? It seems that a technologically driven world will not automatically give us the fulfilment of a purpose and a meaningful life. This better world, which we are now trying to create using technology, does it not depend much more on the ability to do something with ourselves, on the ability to develop ourselves?

The future no one expects is not about the future we are heading for, but the future that is coming towards us. A future that cannot be made by people but one that is shaping us. The trends are visible everywhere. It is a future that cannot be welcomed with methods and expectations from the past, but one that will need entirely new ways of living and understanding. The main misconception in dealing with the future is the idea that everything on earth remains the same, that the human is the only significant factor on earth, that everything can only be understood by looking at physical laws and that there are no influences with an impact on physical reality outside the ingredients of that reality itself. This turns out not to be the case.

For a long time, the power of the earth's magnetic field and its ability to protect appeared to be decreasing by about 10% per century. In 2016, the European Space Agency conducted new research, with its Swarm satellites. This proved that the speed with which the protective layers of the earth's magnetic field are diminishing has increased dramatically. However, the power of the geomagnetic field is not decreasing at the same rate everywhere on earth. In 2016, the decline seemed to be strongest above Brazil [10*]. The faster the earth's magnetic field weakens, the stronger the influence of the heliosphere and the intergalactic winds on earth.

What are the trends which indicate that the future comes towards us in an electromagnetic sense and cannot be made or understood as such in physical phenomena? There are more expressions of inspiration and creativity than ever before, and this is a trend. Unknown viruses and bacteria are appearing more frequently and in greater numbers than ever before, more inventions and more scientific discoveries are being made than ever before. More patents have been applied for and more technological innovations are being made every year than ever before. More people are travelling than ever before. There are more artists, more book publications and more music releases per year than ever before. The list of upward trends continues to expand and now covers almost every aspect of life on earth. What unites all these divergent trends? In any case, whichever way you look at it: more energy. Where does this energy come from?

Study among pedestrians in cities all over the world showed that their pace had increased by an average of 10 percent over ten years. Of the 32 locations studied, Singapore showed the biggest increase of a staggering 30%. Copenhagen ranked second, Madrid third, Berlin seventh, New York eighth and London twelfth [11*]. If the geosphere is decreasing in strength and more energy from that heliospheric environment enters the planet, and there seems to be a direct link between that new energy and everything we do, feel and think, then walking at higher speeds could be one of the symptoms. Is there perhaps a connection between the rise in energy and the increase in polarization, virus mutations, volatility among people and nations and other world trends?

Where does the future actually come from? Will the future, indeed, come in physical form? Is the future merely a reordering of matter with evolution as a kind of guiding and optimizing influence? Or is it perhaps important to look at the future in its pure energetic form? Does the future appear primarily in energy? Is it true that as the geomagnetic field decreases faster in strength and vitality, the influence of the heliosphere and the intergalactic environment increases in strength and vitality on earth? Is it true that we humans and also animals and plants, as unmistakable parts of the electric ecosystem, will react to this? Are most of the changes that take place in essence a response to the changes in the much larger electromagnetic dynamic? Preparing ourselves and tuning our thoughts and actions to an unknown future that works by means of electricity and magnetism may be a challenge, both individually and collectively. However, in the context of all that is brought together it appears to be the most natural thing to do.

Acknowledgements

In an ecosystem everything is interconnected, everything seeks and finds help and most things are accomplished because of the phenomenal power of mutual support. This work is no exception. Therefore, here are some words of appreciation for those who have contributed to it.

First of all, Anne-Marie Meevis. I thank her for her ability to reduce things to their essence - with finesse and sometimes relentlessness. Without her the book would have been at least 400 pages. With the assistance of her fresh energy and support the whole has come into being. I would also like to mention Gerda van Schaik, who has selflessly offered her attention, time, advice and love of language again and again; her commitment was a huge encouragement. Then there is Lydia Funneman with her mastermind and surprising ideas; her expertise, joy in design and creative genius have oxygenated the book. It has been my pleasure to work with Mark Stolk. His unbridled willingness, vigour and ability to translate content into breathtaking composition, form and colour has ensured that the cover conveys the essence of the book. Appreciation also goes to Lianne Wouters, Anna Hannon and Rosamond Rolleston who have been adding their time and effort by way of language arts, attention to detail and enquiring mind qualities.

I hereby extend a posthumous thank-you to Jan Funneman and Fieke Stevens for their unconditional, substantial and active support for every project I have undertaken. Then there are friends, family and colleagues who encouraged me with their sincere interest, enthusiasm, concern and urgency about there being a liveable future. Many thanks, you have been a stimulating influence and part of the inspiration that has enabled this research project to see the light of day.

In addition, there are words of thanks to this planet for her patience with the restive human race. To conclude, I would like to thank the future for its hope and the fact that everything is possible in the future, every second of every day...

List of Abbreviations and Synonyms

Abbreviations

EMF — Electromagnetic frequency
EMST — Electromagnetic signal transference

Hz — Hertz
KHz — Kilohertz
MHz — Megahertz
GHz — Gigahertz
THz — Terahertz

Synonyms

Earth's magnetic field - Geomagnetic field - Geosphere - Geospheric field - The natural internet of things

Bacterium - microorganism - microbe

References

Introduction

1. Pittman UJ - Biomagnetic responses in potatoes - *Canadian Journal of Plant Science, 52(5): p. 727-733, https://doi.org/10.4141/cjps72-119* – 6 July 1972
2. Takahashi T, Isono K - Electric charge on raindrops grown in warm clouds over the island of Hawaii - *Water research laboratory, faculty of science, Nagoya University, Japan, https://doi.org/10.1111/j.2153-3490.1967.tb01497.x* – 27 January 1967
3. Blakemore RP, Frankel RB - Magnetic navigation in bacteria - *Scientific American p.24-49* – 1981
4. Cazzoli D, Muri RM, Schumacher R, Von Arx S, *et al.* - Theta burst stimulation reduces disability during the activities of daily living in spatial neglect - *Brain: 135; 3426–3439* – 24 July 2012
5. Ashcroft F – Book: The spark of life, electricity in the human body - *Publisher W.W. Norton & Company, New York-London, p. 36-37* – 2012
6. Kuritzky A, Zoldan Y, Hering R, Stoupel R - Geomagnetic activity and the severity of the migraine attack - *Headache, volume 27, issue 2, p. 87-89* - February 1987
7. Stoupel E - Cardiac arrhythmia and geomagnetic activity - *Division of Cardiology, Rabin Medical Center, Petah Tiqwa, Israel, Indian Pacing and Electrophysiology Journal (ISSN 0972-6292), 6(1): p. 49-53* – April 2006
8. Meijer M - En dan nu de migrainevooruitzichten - *Algemeen Dagblad Magazine p. 20-23* – April 2002

Animals, plants and the Earth

1. Volkov AG, Chua LO, *et al.* - Memristors in plants. Plant signalling & behaviour - *PubMed DOI:10.4161/psb.28152* - 24 April 2018
2. Billig S, Geist P – Die Intelligenz der Pflanzen – Online: https://www.deutschlandfunkkultur.de/die-intelligenz-der-pflanzen.1067.de.html?dram:article_id=175600 – 21 February 2010
3. Nirody J, Jinn J, Libby T, et al. - Geckos race across the water's surface using multiple mechanisms - *Current Biology, volume 28, Issue 24, p. 4046-4051 – Online: https://doi.org/10.1016/j.cub.2018.10.064* – 17 December 2018
4. Walker MM - Magnetic orientation and the magnetic sense in arthropods - *PubMed: 9415992 - Experimental Biology Research Group, School of Biological Sciences, University of Auckland, New Zealand p. 187-213* – 1997
5. Nenadovic V, Mrdakovic M, Lazarevic J, *et al.* - Temperature and magnetic field effects on the activity of protocerebral neurosecretory neurons and corpora allata in ceramibyx cerdo L. Larvae – *Siniša Stanković Institute for Biological Research, Bulevar Despota Stefana 142, 11000 Belgrade, Serbia and Montenegro, Arch. Biol. Sci., Belgrade, 57 (1), p. 19-24* – 2005
6. Spadara JA - Electrically stimulated bone growth in animals and man – *Pub Med; 319932 https://www.ncbi.nlm.nih.gov/pubmed/319932* – January/ February 1977
7. Lyons LA – Why do cats purr? – *Scientific American, https://www.scientificamerican.com/article/why-do-cats-purr/* - 27 January 2003

Bees

1. Independent - Ryan Ferguson's story on bees - *The Independent UK* - 22 April 2007
2. Stokroos I, Litinetsky L, van der Want JJL, Ishay JS - Keystone-like crystals in cells of hornet combs – *University of Groningen, the Netherlands, Nature volume 411 issue 6838, p. 654* - 6 July 2001
3. Corbet SA, Beament J, Eisikowitch D - Are electrostatic forces involved in pollentransfer? – *Plant, Cell & Environment, volume 5, issue 2, p. 125-129, https://doi.org/10.1111/1365-3040.ep11571488* – April 1982

4. Greggers U, Koch G, Schmidt V, et al. - Reception and learning of electric fields in bees - *Proceedings of the Royal B Society, 280: 20130528.* *http://dx.doi.org/10.1098/rspb.2013.0528* – 22 May 2013

5. Clarke D, Whitney H, Sutton G, Robert D - Detection and learning of floral electric fields by bumblebees – *Science, volume 340, issue 6128, p.66-69, DOI:10.1126/science.1230883* – 5 April 2013

6. Clarke D, Morley E, Rober D - The bee, the flower, and the electric field: electric ecology and aerial electroreception – *Springer, J Comp Physiol A (2017) 203: p. 737–748, DOI:10.1007/s00359-017-1176-6* – 2017

7. Rycroft M, Israelsson S, Price C - The global atmospheric electric circuit, solar activity and climate change – *Elsevier Science Ltd, Pergamon, Journal of Atmospheric and Solar-Terrestrial Physics p. 1563–1576* – 14 June 2000

8. Bowker GE, Crenshaw HC - Electrostatic forces in wind-pollination, Part 1: measurement of the electrostatic charge on pollen – *EPA, US Environmental Protection Agency, Elsevier Science Ltd, New York, NY, 41(8): p. 1587-1595* – 3 January 2007

9. Jackson CW, McGonigle DF - Effect of surface material on electrostatic charge of house-flies (Musca domestica L.) as they walk on a dielectric surface - *Division of Biodiversity and Ecology, School of Biological Sciences, Biomedical Sciences Building, Bassett Crescent East, University of Southampton, PMID: 11975185, DOI:10.1002/ps.463* – April 2002

10. Lihoreau M, Raine NE - Bee positive: the importance of electroreception in pollinator cognitive ecology - *Frontiers in Psychology, Comparative Psychology, volume 4, article 445, DOI:10.3389/fpsyg.2013.00445* – 17 July 2013

11. Brown EA - Hoe bijenseks door de mens wordt verpest - *National Geographic* – 14 september 2018

12. Gould JL, Kirschvink JL, Deffeyes KS, Brines ML - Orientation of demagnetized bees – *Princeton University USA and Rockefeller University New York USA J, exp. Biol., 86 p. 1-8, Printed in Great Britain* – 1980

13. Eskov EK, Sapozhnikov AM - Bees generate electromagnetic signals with a modulation frequency between 180 and 250 Hz when they do their communication dances – 1974

14. Hernandez CU, Jongeling C, Rouw H, van Loon M – Sham or reason for concern? The influences of electromagnetic fields on honeybees – *Student report commissioned by the Science shop of Wageningen UR, the Netherlands p. 38* – November/ December 2010

15. Colin ME, Chauzy S - Measurement of Electric Charges Carried by Bees: Evidence of Biological Variations – *Journal of Bioelectricity, volume 10, 1991, issue 1-2, p. 17-32, DOI:10.3109/15368379109031397* – 7 July 2009

16. Pro Natura, Thielens A, Bell D, Mortimore DB, *et al.* - Exposure of Insects to high frequency EMF's from 2 to 120 GHz – *Ghent University Belgium, University of California Berkeley USA, University of Suffolk UK, Newbourne Solutions Ltd Woodbridge UK. Charles Sturt University Australia, Scientific Reports (2018) 8:3924, DOI:10.1038/s41598-018-22271-3* - 2 March 2018

17. Liang CH, Chuang CL, Jiang JA, Yang EC - Magnetic sensing through the abdomen of the honey bee – *Sci.Rep. 2016 Mar 23;6:23657, DOI:10.1038/srep23657* – March 2016

18. Lambinet V, Hayden ME, Reigl K, Gomis S, Gries G - Linking magnetite in the abdomen of honey bees to a magnetoreceptive function – *Pub med, Royal society publishing, Simon Fraser University, Burnaby, British Columbia, Canada, DOI:10.1098/rspb.2016.2873* – 29 March 2017

19. Hsu CY, Li CW - Magnetoreception in honeybees – *Science, volume 265, issue 5168, p. 95-97, DOI:10.1126/science.265.5168.95* – 1 July 1994

20. Hsu CY, Ko FY, Li CW, Fann K, Lue JT - Magnetoreception system in honeybees (Apis mellifera) - https://doi.org/10.1371/journal.pone.0000395 – April 2007

21. Von Frisch K – Decoding the language of the Bee – *American association for the advancement of Science, https://www.jstor.org/stable/1738718 - Science new series, volume 185, no 4152* – 23 August 1974

Bacteria

1. Lee BY, Zueger C, Zhang J, Chung WJ, et al. - Virus-based piezoelectric energy generation – *University of California, USA, Nature Nanotechnology, volume 7, p.351–356, https://doi.org/10.1038/nnano.2012.69* – 13 May 2012

2. Poddar S, Khurana S - Geobacter: The Electric Microbe! Efficient Microbial Fuel Cells to Generate Clean, Cheap Electricity - *Indian J Microbiol. p.240–241, DOI:10.1007/s12088-011-0180-8* - June 2011

3. Light S, Ajo-Franklin CM, Portnov DA, Rivera-Lugo R, et al. - A flavin-based extracellular electron transfer mechanism in diverse Gram-positive bacteria – *University of California, Berkeley, Nature. p.140-144, DOI:10.1038/s41586-018-0498-z* – 12 September 2018

4. Klinghardt D - EMF and the potentiation of pathogens and heavy metals: effective mitigation and detox – *Klinghardt Institute, London* – November 2017

5. Larionov SV, Krivenko DV - Effect of electromagnetic radiation of the extremely high frequency millimeter range on thermophilic cultures of bacteria of lactic acid products - *Allerton Press, Inc. Agricult. Sci. (2011) 37: 434, https://doi.org/10.3103/S1068367411050156* – 27 November 2011

6. Caubet R, Pedarros-Caubet F, Chu M, Freye E, et al. - A radio frequency electric current enhances antibiotic efficacy against bacterial biofilms - *DOI:10.1128/AAC.48.12.4662-4664.2004, PMC529182* – 5 December 2004

7. Merriman H, Hegyi CA, Albright-Overton CR, Carlos J, et al. - A comparison of four electrical stimulation types on Staphylococcus aureus growth in vitro – *JRRD, volume 41 number 2 p. 139-146* – March/April 2004

8. Mendoza L – Can electricity kill bacteria? – *California State Science Fair, Project number J1609* – 2013

9. Sankey OF, Dykeman EC - Low Frequency Mechanical Modes of Viral Capsids: An Atomistic Approach – *American Physical Society, Arizona State University, https://doi.org/10.1103/PhysRevLett.100.028101* – 14 January 2008

10. Süel G, Prindle A, Liu J, Asally M, Ly S, Garcia-Ojalvo J - Ion channels enable electrical communication within bacterial communities - *University of California San Diego, University of Warwick Coventry UK and University Pompeu Fabra Barcelona Spain, Nature; 527(7576): p. 59–63. DOI:10.1038/nature15709* – 5 November 2015

11. Widom A, Swain J, Srivastava N - Electromagnetic Signals from Bacterial DNA - *University Boston MA USA, University of Perugia Perugia Italy and North-eastern University Boston MA USA, arXiv:1104.3113 [physics.gen-ph]* – 15 April 2011

12. Blakemore RP, Frankel RB - Magnetotactic Bacteria; bacteriën navigeren op het magnetische veld van de aarde - *Scientific American 245(6):58-65, DOI:10.1038/scientificamerican1281-58* - 24 October 1975

13. Schüler D, Scheffel A, Gruska M, Falvre D, Linaroudis A, Plitzko JM - An acidic protein aligns magnetosomes along a filamentous structure in magnetotactic bacteria - Bacteria sense the Earth's magnetic field - *Max Planck Gesellschaft, Germany published in Nature, DOI:10.1038/nature04382, p. 110-114* – 20 November 2005

14. Muxworthy A, Williams W – Critical superparamagnetic/single-domain grain sizes in interacting magnetite particles: implications for magnetosome crystals – *Imperial College London, Royal Society Interface, p.1207-1212, https://doi.org/10.1098/rsif.2008.0462* - 17 December 2008

15. Li L, Yu P, Wang X, Yu SS, Mathieu J, Yu HQ, Alvarez PJJ - Enhanced biofilm penetration for microbial control by polyvalent phages conjugated with magnetic colloidal nanoparticle clusters (CNCs), Magnets turn viruses into bacteria-killers – *Environ. Sci.:Nano2017, p.1817-1826, DOI:10.1039/C7EN00414A* – 10 May 2017

16. Matsunaga T, Nemoto M, Arakaki A, Tanaka M – Proteomic analysis of irregular, bullet-shaped magnetosomes in the sulphate-reducing magnetotactic

bacterium Desulfovibrio magneticus RS-1 - *Proteomics, volume 9, issue 12 p. 3341-3352, https://doi.org/10.1002/pmic.200800881* – 28 December 2009

17. Katzmann E, Müller FD, Lang C, Messerer M, Winklhofer M, *et al.* - How bacteria break a magnet, Magnetosome chains are recruited to cellular division sites and split by asymmetric septation – *Molecular Microbiology, volume 82, issue 6, p.1316-1329, https://doi.org/10.1111/j.1365-2958.2011.07874.x* – 26 October 2011

18. Nielsen LP, Risgaard-Petersen N, Fossing H, Christensen PB, Sayama M - Electric currents couple spatially separated biogeochemical processes in marine sediment - *Nature 463 p. 1071-1074, https://doi.org/10.1038/nature08790* - 24 February 2010

19. Nealson K, Brahic C – Meet the electric life forms that live on pure energy - *University of Southern California USA, New Scientist, issue 2978* - 19 July 2014

20. Soghomonyan D, Trchounian K, Trchounian A – Millimeter waves or extremely high frequency electromagnetic fields in the environment: what are their effects on bacteria? – *Springer Berlin Heidelberg, Appl Microbiol Biotechnol (2016) 100: 4761. https://doi.org/10.1007/s00253-016-7538-0* - 18 April 2016

21. Alkawareek M, Algwari QT, Laverty G, Gorman SP, *et al.* – Eradication of Pseudomonas aeruginosa Biofilms by Atmospheric Pressure Non-Thermal Plasma, Plasma jet kills superbugs in hospitals, safe enough to use on skin - *Queen's University of Belfast UK, DOI:10.1371/journal.pone.0044289* – 31 August 2012

Cells

1. Vernadsky VI – Book, The biosphere – *Publisher Copernicus, 178 pages, DOI:10.1007/978-1-4612-1750-3, ISBN:978-1-4612-7264-9* – 1926

2. Zhao M, Forrester JV, McCaig CD - A small, physiological electric field orients cell division - *University of Colorado, Boulder, PNAS p.4942-4946, https://doi.org/10.1073/pnas.96.9.4942* – 27 April 1999

3. Glander KE – What (howler) monkeys chew to choose their children's sex – *Duke University, Durham, Magazine; New Scientist, issue 1809* – 22 February 1992

4. Koltzoff NK, Schrader VN - Artificial Control of Sex in the Progeny of Mammals. The electrical beginning of new life; Electric Fertilisation - *Published in Nature magazine* - 1933

5. Schoun P – Preconceptual gender determination in mammals, Electric gender determination, Application of variation in electrochemical potential pellucid zone of the ovocyte – *Gender Science Singapore, Online: http://www.babymethods.com/research.html* – 2019

6. Okuno M, Ishijima SA, Odagri H, Mohri T, Mohri H - Separation of X- and Y-chromosome-bearing murine sperm by free-flow electrophoresis: evaluation of separation using PCR, A bright halo found around fertilization; Success in fertilization: A question of time and electricity – *University of Tokyo, Japan, PMID:1369423, Zoolog.Sci. 1992 Jun;9(3): p.601-606* – June 1992

7. Schoun P – Preconceptual gender determination in mammals, Electric gender determination, Application of variation in electrochemical potential pellucid zone of the ovocyte – *Gender Science Singapore, Online: http://www.babymethods.com/research.html* – 2019

8. Lowry C – The electric embryo: How electric fields mold the embryo's growth pattern and shape – *Centre Science Associates, Washington DC, USA, Journal; 21 century science & technology, volume 12, issue 1 p.56-73* – 5 May 1999

9. Albrecht-Bühler G – Surface extensions of 3T3 cells towards distant infrared light sources, The cells open their eyes - *Northwestern University Medical School, Chicago, Illinois, J Cell Biol. 1991 Aug;114(3): p.493-502, DOI:10.1083/jcb.114.3.493* – 1 January 1991

10. Gurwitsch AG - Über den Begriff des embryonales Feldes – *Springer, Arch.Entw.Mech.Org.51 (1922) p.383–415* – 1922

11. Gurwitsch AG - Die Natur des spezifischen Erregers der Zellteilung – *Springer, Arch.Entw.Mech.Org. 100 (1923) p.11–40* – 1923

12. Kopelman R, Tyner KM, Philbert MA – Nanosized Voltmeter, Enables Cellular-Wide Electric Field Mapping, Human cells have electric fields as powerful as lightning bolts - *University of Michigan Biophys J. volume 93, p.1163–1174, DOI:10.1529/biophysj.106.092452* - 15 August 2007

13. Arber SL, Lin JC – Microwave-induced changes in nerve cells: effects of modulation and temperature – *Bio Electro Magnetics, volume 6, issue 3, p. 257-270, https://doi.org/10.1002/bem.2250060306* - 1985

14. Salford L, Brun AE, Eberhardt JL, Persson B, Malmgren L, Bertil R - Nerve cell damage in mammalian brain after exposure to microwaves from GSM mobile phones – *Lund University Sweden, Environmental Health Perspectives, volume 111, number 7, p. 881-883* – June 2003

15. Blank M, Goodman R - DNA is a fractal antenna in electromagnetic fields - *Columbia University New York USA, Int.J.Radiat.Biol. 2011 Apr; 87(4), p. 409-415, PMID: 21457072 - DOI:10.3109/09553002.2011.538130* – 28 February 2011

16. Romanenko S, Begley R, Harvey AR, Hool L, *et al.* - The interaction between electromagnetic fields at MHz, GHz and THz frequencies with cells, tissues and organisms: risks and potential – *University of Western Australia, Perth, J.R.Soc.Interface, DOI:10.1098/rsif.2017.0585* - 14 August 2017

17. Durant F, Bischof J, Fields C, Morokuma J, LaPalme J, Hoi A, Levin M - The role of early bioelectric signals in the regeneration of planarian anterior/posterior polarity - *Biophysical Journal, volume 116, issue 5 p. 948-961, DOI:10.1016/j.bpj.2019.01.029* – 16 January 2019

18. Lipton B – YouTube - Interview with Dr. Bruce Lipton, The influence of electrosmog on the cells – *Online: https://www.youtube.com/watch?v=olGc3bgoI8w* – 20 April 2017

19. Zothansiama, Zosangzuali M, Lalramdinpuii M, Jagetia GC - Impact of radiofrequency radiation on DNA damage and antioxidants in peripheral blood lymphocytes of humans residing in the vicinity of mobile phone base stations - *Mizoram University Aizawl Mizoram, India Electromag Biol Med.;36(3): p.295-305, DOI:10.1080/15368378.2017.1350584* – 4 August 2017

20. Haltiwanger S - The Electrical Properties of Cancer Cells – *Online: http://www.royalrife.com/haltiwanger1.pdf* - 2002

21. Wilke I - Biological and pathological effects of 2.45 GHz on cells, fertility, brain and behaviour - *ISSN 1437-2606, Umwelt · Medizin · Gesellschaft, nr. 31* – 31 February 2018

22. Haltiwanger S - The Electrical Properties of Cancer Cells – *Online: http://www.royalrife.com/haltiwanger1.pdf* - 2002

23. Lipton B – YouTube - Interview with Dr. Bruce Lipton, The influence of electrosmog on the cells – *Online: https://www.youtube.com/watch?v=olGc3bgoI8w* – 20 April 2017

Higher Spheres

1. Kronberg E, Escoubet P, Masson A – Planets such as Mercury, Earth or Jupiter that have their own magnetic field are protected by the magnetic bubble that it generates – *Max Planck Institute for Solar System Research, Germany, ESA, Space Science, Online: https://m.esa.int/Our_Activities/Space_Science/Observing_Jupiter_to_understand_Earth* - 5 December 2008

2. Halekas J - The Moon and the Magnetotail, The bi-polar energizing of the moon and the moon gets negatively energised by the Earth magneto-tail and positively by the solar-winds – *Online info NASA: https://www.nasa.gov/topics/moonmars/features/magnetotail_080416.html* - 16 April 2008

3. Harada Y - Book: Interactions of Earth's Magnetotail Plasma with the Surface, Plasma, and Magnetic Anomalies of the Moon, About the magneto-tail that charges the moons electric field – *Kyoto University Japan and 'Japan Aerospace Exploration Agency' (JAXA) Publisher Springer Japan, ISBN 978-4-431-56256-6, DOI:10.1007/978-4-431-55084-6* – 2015

4. Westrenen W, Meijer R – Boek: Hoe werkt de aarde? Een nieuwe kijk op het binnenste van onze planeet - *EAN:9789085710677* - April 2009

5. Wieser M, Barabash S, Futaana Y, Holmström M, Bhardwaj A, Sridharan R, *et al.* - First observation of a mini-magnetosphere above a lunar magnetic anomaly using energetic neutral atoms, The evolving lunar-sphere, Small magnetospheres are emerging on the moon – *Geophys. Res. Lett. 37:015103* - 19 November 2010

6. Harada Y - Book: Interactions of Earth's Magnetotail Plasma with the Surface, Plasma, and Magnetic Anomalies of the Moon – *Publisher Springer Japan, ISBN 978-4-431-56256-6, DOI:10.1007/978-4-431-55084-6* - 2015

7. Terada T, Yokota S, Asamura K, Saito Y, Kitamura N, Nishino MN - Biogenic oxygen from Earth transported to the Moon by a wind of magnetospheric ions - *Nature Astronomy 1(2):0026, DOI:10.1038/s41550-016-0026* - 30 January 2017

8. Van Allen JA – Radiation Belts Around the Earth, Discovery of the van Allen radiation belts encircling the Earth – *University of Iowa, Scientific American, volume 200, p. 39-47* – March 1959.

9. Maffei EM - Magnetic field effects on plant growth, development, and evolution – *University Turin Italy, Frontiers in Plant Science 5:445, DOI:10.3389/fpls.2014.00445* – 4 September 2014

10. Vogel T, Simonet P - Zap! Some more bacteria are genetically modified, Lightning; nature's own genetic engineer - *University of Lyon France, New Scientist Magazine issue 2469* – 13 October 2004

11. Arendse MC, Kruyswijk CJ – Orientation of Talitrus saltator Sandhopper to magnetic fields – *Elsevier, Netherlands Journal of Sea Research volume 15, issue 1, p. 23-32, https://doi.org/10.1016/0077-7579(81)90003-X* - October 1981

12. Prolic ZM, Nenadovic V - The influence of a permanent magnetic field on the process of adult emergence in Tenebrio molitor (yellow mealworm beetle) – *Elsevier, Journal of Insect Physiology volume 41, issue 12, p. 1113-1118, https://doi.org/10.1016/0022-1910(95)00061-X* – December 1995

13. Malkemper EP, Tscheulin T, Van Bergen AJ, Vian A, Balian E, Goudeseune L - The impacts of artificial Electromagnetic Radiation on wildlife (flora and fauna) - *Current knowledge overview: a background document to the web conference. A report of the EKLIPSE project* – 2018

14. Semm P - Neurobiological investigation of the magnetic sensitivity of the pineal gland in rodents and pigeons – *Elsevier, Comparative Biochemistry and Physiology Part A: Physiology volume 76, issue 4, p. 683-689, https://doi.org/10.1016/0300-9629(83)90129-9* – 1983

15. Sheldrake R – Book: Dogs that know when their owners are coming home and other unexplained powers of animals - *Publisher: Broadway Books, ISBN-10: 0307885968* – 1999

16. Scott DE – Book: The Electric Sky - *Publisher Mikamar Publishing Portland Oregon, ISBN-10: 0977285111* – 2006

17. Vanselow KH, Ricklefs K – Are solar activity and sperm whale *Physeter macrocephalus* strandings around the North Sea related – *Elsevier bv, Journal of Sea Research 53 (2005) p. 319-327, Forschungs- und Technologiezentrum Westkueste, University of Buesum, Germany* - 7 July 2004

18. Broers D – Book: Solar revolution: why mankind is on the cusp of an evolutary leap – *Publisher Evolver Editions, ISBN: 9781583945049* - 2012

19. Burda H, Begall S, Cerveny J, Neef J, Vojtech O - Magnetic alignment in grazing and resting cattle and deer – *Faculty of biology, University of Duisburg-Essen Germany, Proc Natl Acad Sci USA; 105(36): p. 13451–13455, DOI:10.1073/pnas.0803650105* – 9 September 2008

20. Hartl V, Nováková P, Malkemper EP, Begall S, Hanzal V, Ježek M, Kušta T, Němcová V, Adámková J, Benediktová K, Červený J, Burda H – Dogs prefer to excrete in line with the Earth's magnetic field - *Czech University of Life Sciences Czech Republic, University of Duisburg-Essen Germany, Front Zool. 2013 Dec 27;10(1):80. DOI:10.1186/1742-9994-10-80* – 27 December 2013

21. Shumilov O - Does the Earth's magnetic field cause suicides, Earth magnetic field influences the heartbeat of a fetus - *Institute of North Industrial Ecology Problems Russia, New Scientist Online: https://www.newscientist.com/article/dn13769-does-the-earths-magnetic-field-cause-suicides/* - 24 April 2008

22. Kay RW - Geomagnetic Storms: Association with Incidence of Depression as Measured by Hospital Admission - *The Royal College of Psychiatrists Westbank Clinic, Falkirk Stirlingshire UK published in The British Journal of Psychiatry, volume 164, p. P403-409, https://doi.org/10.1192/bjp.164.3.403* - March 1994

23. Palmer SJ, Rycroft MJ, Cermack M – The impact of solar and geomagnetic activity on human health at the earth's surface – *Surv.Geophys (2006) 27: p. 557-595, DOI:10.1007/s10712-006-9010-7* – 5 July 2006

24. Finkbeiner D, Scolnic DM, Jones DO, Rest A, Pan YC, Chonock R, et al. - The complete light-curve sample of spectroscopically confirmed SNe Ia from Pan-STARRS1 and cosmological constraints from the combined pantheon sample - *Harvard-Smithsonian Centrum voor Astrofysica, The Astrophysical Journal, volume 859, issue 2, article id. 101, 28 pp DOI:10.3847/1538-4357/aab9bb* - 9 November 2010

Birds

1. Badger M , Ortega-Jimenez VM, von Rabenau L, Smiley A, Dudley R - Electrostatic Charge on Flying Hummingbirds and Its Potential Role in Pollination - *PLoSONE10(9):e0138003, DOI:10.1371/journal.pone.0138003* – 30 September 2015

2. Fransson T, Kullberg C, Henshaw I, Jakobsson S, Johansson P – Fuelling decisions in migratory birds: geomagnetic cues override the seasonal effect, Birds use earth magnetic field to plan migration routes – *Stockholm University, Proc Biol Sci.; 274(1622): p. 2145–2151, DOI:10.1098/rspb.2007.0554* - 7 September 2007

3. Hunt S, Cuthill IC, Swaddle JP, Bennett ATD - Ultraviolet vision and band-colour preferences in female zebra finches,Taeniopygia guttata – *University of Bristol, Anim. Behav., 54, p. 1383–1392* - 8 April 1996

4. Mouritsen H, Liedvogel M – Cryptochromes, a potential magnetoreceptor: what do we know and what do we want to know? Robins can see Earth's magnetic field which allows them to navigate - *University of Oldenburg, Lund University Sweden, J. R. Soc. Interface (2010) 7, S147–S162, DOI:10.1098/rsif.2009.0411* – 11 November 2009

5. Niessner C, Denzau S, Stapput K, Ahmad M, Peich L, - Magnetoreception: activated cryptochrome 1a concurs with magnetic orientation in birds – *J.R.Soc.Interface 10:20130638, DOI:org/10.1098/rsif.2013.0638* – 6 November 2013

6. Ritz T, Thalau P, Phillips JB, Wiltschko R - Resonance effects indicate a radical-pair mechanism for avian magnetic compass – *University of California USA, Goethe-University Frankfurt am Main Germany, Virginia Tech. Blacksburg USA - Nature Publishing Group, volume 429* – 13 May 2004

7. Balmori A - Effects of the electromagnetic fields of phone masts on a population of White Stork (Ciconia ciconia), Valladolid, Spain – *Journal Electromagnetic Biology and Medicine, volume 24 (2005), issue 2, p. 109-119, https://doi.org/10.1080/15368370500205472* – March 2004

8. Kavokin K, Chernetsov N, Pakhomov A, Bojarinova J, Kobylkov D, Namoozov B - Magnetic orientation of garden warblers (Sylvia borin) under 1.4 MHz radiofrequency magnetic field – *Journal of the Royal Society Interface, volume 11, issue 97, https://doi.org/10.1098/rsif.2014.0451* – 6 August 2014

9. Engels S, Schneider NL, Hore PJ, Mouritsen H - Anthropogenic electromagnetic noise disrupts magnetic compass orientation in a migratory bird – *University of Oldenburg Germany and University of Oxford UK, Nature 2014 May 15;509(7500):353-6. DOI:10.1038/nature13290* – 15 May 2014

10. Kordas D - Birds and Trees of Northern Greece: Changes since the Advent of 4G Wireless – *PDF online: https://einarflydal.files.wordpress.com/2017/08/kordas-birds-and-trees-of-northern-greece-2017-final.pdf* – 28 June 2017
11. Wiltschko W, Wiltschko R, Freire R - The magnetic compass of domestic chickens, Gallus gallus - *Journal of experimental biology, DOI:10.1242/jeb.004853* – 2007
12. Piersma T, Aelst R van, Kurk K, Berkhout H, Maas LRM - A new pressure sensory mechanism for prey detection in birds: the use of principles of seabed dynamics – *The Royal Society, Proc. R. Soc.Lond.B. (1998) 265, p. 1377-1383, DOI:10.1098/rspb.1998.0445* – 16 April 1998
13. Hunt S, Cuthill IC, Swaddle JP, Bennett ATD - Ultraviolet vision and band-colour preferences in female zebra finches, Taeniopygia guttata – *University of Bristol UK, PMID:9521795, Anim. Behav., 1997, 54, p. 1383–1392* - 6 April 1996

Aquatic animals

1. Balcombe J – Book: What a fish knows: The inner lives of our underwater cousins - *Scientific American / Farrar, Straus and Giroux, ISBN-13: 978-0374537098* – 2016
2. Fields RD – The shark's electric sense. An astonishingly sensitive detector of electric fields helps sharks zero in on prey – *Scientific American p. 74-81* – August 2007
3. Murray RW - Receptor mechanisms in the ampullae of lorenzini of elasmobranch Fishes – *University of Birmingham UK, Cold Spring Harbor Symposia on Quantitative Biology 30: p. 233-243, DOI:10.1101/SQB.1965.030.01.026* – 1965
4. Fields RD – The shark's electric sense. An astonishingly sensitive detector of electric fields helps sharks zero in on prey – *Scientific American, p. 74-81* – August 2007
5. Nelson ME – Electric Fish - *University of Illinois USA, Curr Biol. 21(14): p. R528-R529. DOI:10.1016/j.cub.2011.03.045* – 26 July 2011
6. Carlson B, Hasan SM, Hollmann M, Miller DB, Harmon LJ, Arnegard ME - Brain evolution triggers increased diversification of electric fishes – *Science, 29 April 2011, volume 332, issue 6029, p. 583-586, DOI:10.1126/science.1201524* - 28 April 2013
7. Bullock TH, Hamstra RH, Scheich H, Comp HJ – The jamming avoidance response of high frequency electric fish - *Physiol. (1972) 77: 1, https://doi.org/10.1007/BF00696517* – 1972
8. Feng AS – Electric organs and electroreceptors – *in Comparative Animal Physiology, 4th ed., ed. CL Prosser, 217-34 (New York: John Wiley and Sons)* - 1991
9. Vanselow KH, Ricklefs K – Are solar activity and sperm whale *Physeter macrocephalus* strandings around the North Sea related – *Elsevier bv, Journal of Sea Research 53 (2005) p. 319-327, Forschungs- und Technologiezentrum Westkueste, University of Buesum, Germany* - 7 July 2004
10. Eder SHK, Cadiou H, Muhamad A, McNaughton PA, Kirschvink JL, Winklhofer M - Magnetic characterization of isolated candidate vertebrate magnetoreceptor cells - *Proceedings of the National Academy of Sciences USA, 109(30), 12022-12027, DOI:10.1073/pnas.1205653109* – 2012
11. Balayev LA - The Behavior of Ecologically Different Fish in Electric Fields II, Threshold of Anode Reaction and Tetanus - *Journal of Ichthyology 21(1): p.134-143* – 1980
12. Formicki K, Winnicki A - Reactions of Fish Embryos and Larvae to Constant Magnetic Fields - *Italian Journal of Zoology, volume 65, issue sup1, p. 479-482, https://doi.org/10.1080/11250009809386870* – 28 August 1997
13. Li Y, Liu X, Liu K, Miao W, Zhou C, Wu H - Extremely Low-Frequency Magnetic Fields Induce Developmental Toxicity and Apoptosis in Zebrafish (Danio rerio) Embryos - *Biological Trace Element Research, vol. 162, no. 1, p. 324-332, DOI:10.1007/s12011-014-0130-5* – 2014
14. Slater M, Fisher C, – Electromagnetic field study. Effects of Electromagnetic Fields on Marine Species: a literature review – *Oregon Wave Energy Trust, 0905-00-001* – 1 September 2010

15. Westerberg H, Langenfelt I - Sub-sea power cables and the migration behaviour of the European eel – *Fisheries Management and Ecology volume 15, issue 5-6, p.369-375, https://doi.org/10.1111/j.1365-2400.2008.00630.x* – 22 October 2008
16. Hanke W, Dehnhardt G, Czech-Damal NU, Manger P - Seal scan see with electroreceptive whiskers – *University of Rostock Germany, Journal of experimental Biology, Online BBC Science & Environment; https://www.bbc.com/news/10287564* - 11 June 2010
17. Lohmann K, Boles L, Avens L - Use of multiple orientation cues by juvenile loggerhead sea turtles Caretta caretta – *University of North Carolina, Journal of Experimental Biology, 206: p. 4317-4325, DOI:10.1242/jeb.00657* - 6 January 2003
18. Godfrey-Smith P – The mind of an octopus; eight smart limbs plus a big brain add up to a weird and wonderous kind of intelligence - *Scientific American, Neuroscience, Published by arrangement with Farrar, Straus and Giroux, LLC (U.S.), HarperCollins (U.K.), Online: https://www.scientificamerican.com/article/the-mind-of-an-octopus/* - 1 January 2017
19. Oellermann M - Blue Blood on Ice: Cephalopod haemocyanin function and evolution in a latitudinal cline - *University of Tasmania, DOI:10.13140/RG.2.1.1283.3442* - February 2015
20. Gonzalez-Bellido P, Wardill T, Hanlon R, Crook RJ - Neural control of tuneable skin iridescence in squid - *Proceedings of the Royal Society B: Biological Sciences 279(1745): p. 4243-4252, DOI:10.1098/rspb.2012.1374* – 27 August 2012
21. Bedore CN, Kajiura S, Johnsen S - Freezing behaviour facilitates bioelectric crypsis in cuttlefish faced with predation risk - *Duke University, NC, USA, Proc.R.Soc.B, volume 282, DOI:10.1098/rspb.2015.1886* – 2 December 2015

Frogs

1. Galvani L - De Viribus Electricitatis in Motu Musculari, the effect of atmospheric electricity on dead frogs – *Smithsonian Libraries, Online Viewing: https://library.si.edu/digital-library/book/aloysiigalvanid00galv* – 1791
2. Geim AK, Berry MV, Boamfa M – Of flying frogs and levitrons – *University of Nijmegen, The Netherlands and Wills Physics Laboratory Bristol UK, Eur. J. Phys. 18 (1997) p. 307–313* – 4 June 1997
3. Neurath, PW - High gradient magnetic field inhibits embryonic development of frogs – *Nature, volume 219, p.1358–1359, https://doi.org/10.1038/2191358a0* - 1968
4. Catacuzzenoa L, Orfeib F, Di Micheleb A, *et al.* – Energy harvesting from a bio cell – *Elsevier Ltd, Nano Energy 56 (2019) p 823-827* - December 2018
5. Nuccitelli R - Endogenous electric fields in embryos during development, regeneration and wound healing - *RPN Research, New Britain USA, Radiat Prot Dosimetry, 2003;106(4):375-83, DOI:10.1093/oxfordjournals.rpd.a006375* – 1 October 2003
6. Severini M, Bosco L, Alilla R, Loy M, Bonori M, Giuliani L, Bedini A, Giliberti C, Palomba R, Pesolillo S, Giacomozzi E, Castellano AC.- Delayed maturation of Xenopus laevis (Daudin) tadpoles exposed to a weak ELF magnetic field, sensitivity to small variations of magnetic fluxdensity - *Tuscia University Italy, Int.J.Radiat.Biol.;86(1):37-46, DOI:10.3109/09553000903137687* – 13 January 2010
7. Broomhall M, UNESCO - Exodus of species from Mount Nardi Australia as a result of applying an increasing amount of electromagnetic technology (transmission masts) – *Online PDF: http://emraware.com/Documents/Mt%20Nardi%20Wildlife%20Report%20to%20UNESCO.pdf – Unesco and IUCN* – August 2016
8. Balmori A - Mobile Phone Mast Effects on Common Frog (Rana temporaria) Tadpoles: The City Turned into a Laboratory – *Electromagn.Biol.Med.; 29(1-2):31-5, DOI:10.3109/15368371003685363* – June 2010

Plants

1. Chalmers JA, Pasquill F - The electric charges on single raindrops and snowflakes - *Proceedings of the Physical Society, volume 50, number 1* – 1938
2. Takahashi T, Isono K - Electric charge on raindrops grown in warm clouds over the island of Hawaii - *Tellus, 19:3, p.420-431, DOI:10.3402/tellusa.v19i3.9811* - 27 January 1967
3. Mindell E – Book: The happiness effect, the positive benefits of negative ions – *Garden City Park New York USA: Square One Publishers, ISBN 9780757004223* – 2016
4. Jayaratne ER, Ling X, Morawska L - Role of Vegetation in enhancing radon concentration and ion production in the atmosphere - *Queensland University of Technology, Brisbane, QLD, Australia, Environ Sci Technol. 2011 Aug 1;45(15):6350-5, DOI:10.1021/es201152g* – 14 July 2011
5. Ashcroft F – Book: The spark of life. Electricity in the human body - *Publisher W.W. Norton & Company, New York-London, p. 36-37* – 2012
6. Mershin A, Zhang, Love C – Sensor system runs on electricity generated by trees. Circuit for tree-electricity – *MIT Tech Talk, volume 53, nr.3 p. 4* – 24 September 2008
7. Ursem B – Dierckx-Lecture about the link between electricity and trees - *Nederlandse Dendrologische Vereniging* - 2008
8. Ortega VM, Dudley R - Spiderweb deformation induced by electrostatically charged insects – *University of California Berkeley, Sci.Rep.;3:2108, DOI:10.1038/srep02108* - July 2013
9. Davies E - Electrical Signals in Plants: Facts and Hypotheses – *North Carolina State University, Research Gate, DOI:10.1007/978-3-540-37843-3_17* – January 2006
10. Hedrich R, Salvador-Recatala V, Dreyer I - Electrical Wiring and Long-Distance Plant Communication – *University of Würzburg Germany, Trends Plant Sci.;21(5): p.376-387. DOI:10.1016/j.tplants.2016.01.016* - 1 May 2016
11. Mousavi SA, Chauvin A, Pascaud F, Farmer EE - Glutamate receptor-like genes mediate leaf-to-leaf wound signalling. Plant cells talk with electric signals too. Scientists listened into the electric signals of a wounded plant - *University of Lausanne Switzerland, Nature;500(7463): p. 422-426, DOI:10.1038/nature12478* – 22 August 2013
12. Canales J, Henriquez-Valencia C, Brauchi S - The integration of electrical signals originating in the root of vascular Plants – *Frontiers in Plant Science, volume 6, article 2173, DOI:10.3389/fpls.2017.02173* - 10 January 2018
13. Choi WG, Hilleary R, Swanson SJ, Kim SH, Gilroy S - Rapid, long-distance electrical and calcium signalling in plants - *Department of Botany University of Wisconsin-Madison USA, Annu Rev Plant Biol. 2016 Apr 29;67: p.287-307, DOI:10.1146/annurev-arplant-043015-112130* - 14 September 2016
14. Sinicina N, Martinovs A, Skromulis A – Amount of air ions depending on indoor plant activity - *Environment. Technology. Resources, Rezekne, Latvia, Proceedings of the 10th International Scientific and Practical Conference, volume II, p. 267-273, DOI:10.17770/etr2015vol2.247* – June 2015
15. Kim B, Chun K – Electrical stimulation and effects on plant growth in hydroponics – *University of Daegu Korea Journal of Engineering and Applied Sciences 12 (17): p. 4396-4399, ISSN:1816-949X, Medwell Journals* – 2017
16. Magone I - The effect of electromagnetic radiation from the Skrunda Radio Location Station on Spirodela polyrhiza (L.) Schleiden cultures – *Elsevier, Science of The Total Environment, volume 180, issue 1, p. 75-80, https://doi.org/10.1016/0048-9697(95)04922-3* – 2 February 1996.
17. Selga T, Selga M - Response of the Pinus Sylvestris L. needles to electromagnetic fields. Cytological and ultrasructural aspects - *Science of The Total Environment 180(1): p. 65-73, DOI:10.1016/0048-9697(95)04921-5* – February 1996
18. Roux D, Vian A, Girard S, Bonett P, Paladian F, Davies E, Ledoigt G - Electromagnetic fields (900MHz) evoke consistent molecular responses in tomato plants - *Physiologia Plantarum 128: p. 283–288, DOI:10.1111/j.1399-3054.2006.00740.x* – 21 March 2006

19. Halgamuge MN, Yak SK, Eberhardt JL - Reduced growth of soybean seedlings after exposure to weak microwave radiation from GSM 900 mobile phone and base station - *University of Melbourne Victoria Australia, Bioelectromagnetics, 2015 Feb;36(2): p. 87-95, DOI:10.1002/BEM.21890* – 21 January 2015
20. Haggerty K - Adverse influence of radio frequency background on trembling aspen seedlings (trees) – *Hindawi Publishing Corporation International Journal of Forestry Research, volume 2010, Article ID 836278, 7 pages DOI:10.1155/2010/836278* - 17 February 2010
21. Farmer T, Ferraz de Oliveira R - The de-coding of plants' electrical signals has begun! Phytl (plant electrical signal capturing device) signs experimental results – *Online: http://www.phytlsigns.com/the-de-coding-of-plants-electrical-signals-has-begun/* - 3 November 2016
22. Wohlleben P – Book: Das geheime Leben der Bäume, was sie fühlen, wie sie kommunizieren, die Entdeckung einer verborgenen Welt (The hidden life of trees) – *Ludwig Verlag, Verslagsgruppe Random House GmbH, München, Germany, ISBN: 978-3-453-28067-0* – 2015
23. Robert D, Clarke D, Whitney H, Sutton G - Detection and learning of floral electric fields by bumblebees - *Science New York USA, 340(6128), DOI:10.1126/science.1230883* – 5 April 2013
24. Occhipinti A, De Santis A, Maffei ME - Magnetoreception: an unavoidable step for plant evolution? Plants respond to the earth magnetic field - *Trends Plant Sci. 19, 1–4. DOI:10.1016/j.tplants.2013.10.007* – January 2014
25. Maffei ME - Magnetic field effects on plant growth, development, and evolution – *University Turin Italy, Frontiers in Plant Science 5:445, DOI:10.3389/fpls.2014.00445* – 4 September 2014

Humans

1. Popp FA Chang JJ, Fisch J – Book: Biophotons – *Springer 414 pages, DOI:10.1007/978-94-017-0928-6, ISBN 978-90-481-5033-5* - 1998
2. Popp FA, Beloussov L – Book: Intergrative biophysics, biophoyonics – *Publisher Springer NL 504 pages, ISBN 978-90-481-6228-4, DOI:10.1007/978-94-017-0373-4* - 2010
3. Newton M, Peng K, Sonera E - Electromechanical Properties of Bones – *Math 485, Online: https://www.math.arizona.edu/~gabitov/teaching/131/math_485_585/* - 5 April 2013
4. Price CT - Exercising to spark bone growth - *Institute for Better Bone Health, Online: https://www.wendiepett.com/exercising-to-spark-bone-growth/* - 5 June 2013
5. Mortazavi SMJ, Rahimi S, Talebi A, Soleimani A, Rafati A - Survey of the Effects of Exposure to 900 MHz Radiofrequency Radiation Emitted by a GSM Mobile Phone on the Pattern of Muscle Contractions in an Animal Model – *University of medical sciences Shiraz Iran, J Biomed Phys Eng.; 5(3): p. 121–132* – 1 September 2015
6. Abramson HA, Moyer LS – The electrical charge of mammalian red blood cells – *Biological Laboratory, Cold Springs Harbor, Long Island USA, Journal of General Physiology p. 601-607, DOI:10.1085/jgp.19.4.601* – 21 August 1935
7. Martin H, Rozman D, McCraty R, Rozman D – Book: Heart Intelligence: Connecting with the Intuitive Guidance of the Heart - *Waterfront Digital Press, 270 pages, ISBN-13: 978-1943625437* – February 2016
8. Crile G, Glasser O, Quiring DP - The heart and the red blood cells as generator and distributors of static electricity – *The Ohio State University, Ohio Journal of Science: volume 41, issue 5, p. 347-356* - September 1941
9. Smith CW - Elektromagnetische velden en het endocriene systeem – *TIG jaargang 23, deel1: Het regulatiesysteem, Inzichten p.71-83* – 1 March 1992
10. Lazetic B, Kozarcic T, Stankov K - The effect of low-frequency electromagnetic fields on the neuroendocrine system - *Medicinski fakultet Kroatia, Novi Sad, Med. Pregl., 50: p. 357-362* – September/ October 1997

11. Johnson RL, Wilson CG - A review of vagus nerve stimulation as a therapeutic intervention – *Loma Linda University CA USA, Dovepress Journal of Inflammation Research 2018:11, p. 203–213* – November 2018

12. Pal F, Heesakkers JPFA, Bemmelmans BLH - Current opinion on the working mechanisms of neuromodulation in the treatment of lower urinary tract dysfunction – *Radbout University Nijmegen, Chapter 3, Current Opinion in Urology 2006; 16(4):261-7, p.19-34* – 11 October 2006

13. Schrenzel J, Kraus KH - Leucocytes kill bacteria and pathogenic fungi by electrocution. The immune system uses electrocution in healing the body – *University Hospital Geneva Switzerland - Science & Vie Magazine, issue 972, p. 44* – September 1998

14. Marshall TG, Rumann Heil TJ - Electrosmog and autoimmune disease – *Springer, Immunol Res (2017) 65: p.129–135, DOI:10.1007/s12026-016-8825-7* – 13 July 2016

15. Bushdid C, Magnasco MO, Vosshall LB - Human Nose Can Detect a Trillion Smells – *Science (SCP Williams), Online: https://www.sciencemag.org/news/2014/03/human-nose-can-detect-trillion-smells* – 20 March 2014

16. McGann J - Poor human olfaction is a 19th-century myth – *Rutgers University Piscataway USA, Science;356(6338), DOI:10.1126/science.aam7263* – 12 May 2017

17. McCutcheon M, Walmsley D, Epps W – Book: The compass in your Nose and other astonishing facts – *Publisher Tarcher, 193 pages, ISBN-13: 978-0874775440* – 1987

18. Reppert S, Foley LE, Gegear RJ - Human cryptochrome exhibits light-dependent magneto-sensitivity – University of Massachusetts - *Nature Communications, volume 2, article number: 356, https://doi.org/10.1038/ncomms1364* - 21 June 2011

19. Tomatis AA – Book: The conscious ear - *Station Hill Press; 1st US - 1st Printing edition ISBN-10: 0882681087* – 1 March 1992

20. Rea WJ, Pan Y, Fenyves EJ, Sujisawa L, Suyama H, Samadi N, Ross GH - Electromagnetic Field Sensitivity - *Journal of Bioelectricity, volume 10, issue 1-2, https://doi.org/10.3109/15368379109031410* – 1991.

21. Feldman YD, Puzenko A, Ben Ishai P, Caduff A, *et al.* - Human skin as arrays of helical antennas in the millimeter and submillimeter wave range – *The Hebrew University Jerusalem and Ariel University, both in Israel, DOI:10.1103/PhysRevLett.100.128102* – 27 March 2018

22. Zhao M, Penninger J, McCaig C – To heal a wound turn up the voltage - *University of Aberdeen, Scotland, New Scientist Magazine issue 2562* - May 2006.

23. Verbundt J – Magnetoencefalogram, hoe haal je het in en uit je hersens - *MEG-centrum KNAW Amsterdam* - 1996

24. Lang SB, Marino AA, Berkovic G, Fowler M, Abreo KD – Piezoelectricity in the human pineal gland – *Elsevier, Bioelectrochemistry and Bioenergetics 41, p.191-195* – 16 August 1996

25. Bosman S – Research project on the role of the pineal gland as an intermediary between the physical and metaphysical world of experience - *Medical biologist, independent brain and consciousness researcher, Attribution Non-Commercial (BY-NC)* – 2000

26. Lipnicki D – An association between geomagnetic activity and dream bizarreness. Sweet dreams are made of geomagnetic activity – *Elsevier Ltd, Australia, Journal reference: Medical Hypotheses, volume 73, issue 1, p. 115-117, DOI:10.1016/j.mehy.2009.01.047* – July 2009

27. McFadden JJ, Pockett S - The Conscious mind is an electromagnetic field, from the paper, "synchronous firing and its influence on the brain's electromagnetic field: evidence for an electromagnetic field theory of consciousness" – *University of Surrey UK, Journal of Consciousness Studies* - 16 May 2002

Consequences for Animals and Plants

1. Larionov SV, Krivenko DV, Avdeenko AV - Effect of electromagnetic radiation of the extremely high frequency millimeter range on technological properties of milk - *Russ. Agricult. Sci. (2012) 38: 72, https://doi.org/10.3103/S1068367412010144* – 9 February 2011
2. Cucurachia S, Tamisa WLM, Vijver MG, Peijnenburg WJGM, Bolte JFB, de Snoo GR - A review of the ecological effects of radiofrequency electromagnetic fields (RF-EMF) – *Leiden University NLElsevier, Environment International 51; p. 116–140* – January 2013
3. Meijer M - En dan nu de migrainevooruitzichten - *Algemeen Dagblad Magazine p. 20-23* – April 2002.
4. D'Andrea JA, Thomas A, Hatcher DJ - Rhesus monkey behavior during exposure to high-peak-power 5.62-GHz microwave pulses - *Bioelectromagnetics 15(2): p. 163-176, DOI:10.1002/bem.2250150207* – 1994
5. Greenberg B, Bindokas VP, Frazier MJ, Gauger JR - Response of honey bees, Apis mellifera, to high-voltage transmission lines - *Environmental Entomology 10(5): 600-610* – 1981
6. Warnke U - Effects of electric charges on honeybees – *University of Saarbrucken Germany, Journal Beeworld, volume 57, number 2* - 1976
7. Korall H, Leucht T, Martin H - Bursts of magnetic fields induce jumps of misdirection in bees by a mechanism of magnetic resonance – *Springer-Verlag, Journal of Comparative Physiology A, volume 162, issue 3, p. 279–284, https://doi.org/10.1007/BF00606116* – May 1988
8. Walker MM, Bitterman ME - Attached magnets impair magnetic-field discrimination by honey-bees – *University of Hawaii Honolulu USA, The Company of Biologists Limited, J. exp. Biol. 141, p. 447-451* – 13 July 1989
9. Prolić, ZM, Jovanović Z - Influence of magnetic field on the rate of development of honey bee preadult stage - *Periodicum Biologorum 88, p. 187-188* – 1986
10. Bindokas VP, Gauger JR, Greenberg B - Mechanism of biological effects observed in honey bees (Apis mellifera, L.) hived under extra-high-voltage transmission lines: implications derived from bee exposure to simulated intense electric fields and shocks – *Bio Electro Magnetics, volume 9, issue 3, p. 285-301, https://doi.org/10.1002/bem.2250090310* – 1988
11. Bindokas VP, Gauger JR, Greenberg B - Laboratory investigations of the electrical characteristics of honey bees and their exposure to intense electric fields - *University of Illinois at Chicago USA, Bioelectromagnetics;10(1): p.1-12* – 1989
12. Odemer R, Odemer F - Effects of radiofrequency electromagnetic radiation (RF-EMF) on honey bee queen development and mating success – 3 October 2018
13. Sheperd S, *et al.* - Extremely Low Frequency Electromagnetic Fields impair the Cognitive and Motor Abilities of Honey Bees – 21 May 2018
14. Taye RR, Deka MK, Borkataki S, Panda S - Effect of electromagnetic radiation of cell phone tower on development of Asiatic honey bee, Apis cerana F. (Hymenoptera: Apidae) – 26 July 2018
15. El-Halabi N, Achkar R, Haidar GA - The Effect of Cell Phone Radiations on the Life Cycle of Honeybees – July 2013
16. Kumar NR, Sangwan S, Badotra P - Exposure to cell phone radiations produces biochemical changes in worker honey bees – 2011
17. Sainudeen Sahib S - Impact of mobile phones on the density of honeybees - 9 February 2011.
18. Sharma VP, Kumar NR - Changes in honeybee behaviour and biology under the influence of cellphone radiations – 25 May 2010.
19. Favre D - Mobile phone-induced honeybee worker piping – 8 april 2010
20. Kuhn J - Are mobile phones wiping out our bees? Colony Collapse Disorder CCD – 5 April 2007
21. Kuhn J, Kimmel S, Harst W, Stever H - Electromagnetic Radiation: Influences on Honeybees (Apis mellifera) – 2007
22. Stever H, Kuhn J, Harst W, Kimmel S - Change in behaviour of the honeybee Apis mellifera during electromagnetic exposure, follow-up study – 2007

23. Harst W, Kuhn J, Stever H - Can electromagnetic exposure cause a change in behaviour? Studying possible non-thermal influences on honey bees – 2006

24. Keener K - Zapping fruits and vegetables with electricity kills bacteria instantly - *Purdue University, West Lafayette USA, Online (I Chant): https://www.themarysue.com/zapping-fruits-and-vegetables-with-electricity-could-kill-bacteria-instantly-video/* - 17 April 2013

25. Balmori A, Waldmann-Selsam C, Balmori-de la Puente A, Breunig H - Radiofrequency radiation injures trees around mobile phone base stations – *Sci.Total.Environ. 2016 Dec 1;572: p. 554-569. DOI:10.1016/j.scitotenv.2016.08.045* – 24 August 2016

26. Breunig H - Tree damage caused by mobile phone base stations, an observation guide - *Online: https://ehtrust.org/tree-damage-caused-mobile-phone-base-stations-observation-guide-helmut-breunig/* - March 2017

27. Grundler W, Keilmann F, Putterlik V, Strube D - Resonant-like dependence of yeast growth rate on microwave frequencies – *Max Planck Institut Stuttgart Germany, Br.J.Cancer 45, suppl. V, 206* - 1982

28. Grundler W, Keilmann F - Sharp Resonances in yeast growth prove nonthermal sensitivity to microwaves - *American Physical Society, Phys. Rev. Lett. 51, 1214, https://doi.org/10.1103/PhysRevLett.51.1214* – September 1983

29. Tricas T, Gill A – Effects of EMF's from undersea powercables on elasmobranchs and other marine species – *US Department of the Interior, Bureau of Ocean Energy Management, Regulation and Enforcement Pacific OCS Region, Normandeau Associates OCS Study Boemre* – May 2011

30. Balmori A, Hallberg Ö - The urban decline of the house sparrow (Passer domesticus): a possible link with electromagnetic radiation - *Electromagn Biol Med. 2007;26(2): p.141-51, DOI:10.1080/15368370701410558* - 2007

31. Everaert J, Bauwens D - A possible effect of electromagnetic radiation from mobile phone base stations on the number of breeding House Sparrows (Passer domesticus) – *Electromagn.Biol.Med.;26(1): p. 63-72, DOI:10.1080/15368370701205693* – 2007

32. Marks TA, Ratke CC, English WO - Stray voltage and developmental, reproductive and other toxicology problems in dogs, cats and cows: a discussion - *Allegan Study Group Kalamazoo USA, Vet Hum Toxicol.;37(2): p.163-72* – April 1995

33. Loscher W, Kas G - Extraordinary behaviour disorders in cows in proximity to transmission stations - *Translated from German language. Der Praktische Tierarz 79 (5): 4377 444* – 1998

34. Galvin MJ, McRee DI, Hall CA, Thaxton JP, Parkhurst CR - Humoral and cell-mediated immune function in adult Japanese Quail following exposure to 2,45 GHz microwave radiation during embryogeny - *Bioelectromagnetics.;2(3): p. 269-278* – 1981

35. Balmori A, Soya, Martínez - The Effects of Microwaves on the Trees and Other Plants - *Valladolid; Spain* – December 2003

36. El-Khawas S - Effect of electric powerlines stress on growth, some metabolic activities and yield of maize (maïs) - *The Egyptian Society of Experimental Biology Egypt. J. Exp.Biol.(Bot.), 8(2): p. 151–159* – 2012

37. Guerra PA, Gegear RJ, Reppert SM - A magnetic compass aids monarch butterfly migration – *Macmillan Publishers Limited, Nature Communications 5:4164, DOI:10.1038/ncomms5164* – 19 May 2014

38. Halgamuge MN - Review: Weak radiofrequency radiation exposure from mobile phone radiation on plants – *Taylor & Francis Group, Department of Electrical and Electronic Engineering, the University of Melbourne Parkville Victoria Australia, Electromagnetic Biology and Medicine http://dx.doi.org/10.1080/15368378.2016.1220389* – 6 May 2016

39. Kordas D - Birds and Trees of Northern Greece: Changes since the Advent of 4G Wireless – *PDF online, https://einarflydal.files.wordpress.com/2017/08/kordas-birds-and-trees-of-northern-greece-2017-final.pdf* – 28 June 2017

40. Tricas T, Gill A – Effects of EMF's from undersea powercables on elasmobranchs and other marine species – *US Department of the Interior, Bureau of Ocean Energy Management,*

Regulation and Enforcement Pacific OCS Region, Normandeau Associates OCS Study Boemre – May 2011

41. Hanafy MS, Mohamed HA, El-HadyE A - The effect of low frequency electric fields on the growth characteristic and the protein molecular structure of wheat plants. Exposure to high voltage transmission lines limits plant growth – *Proceeding of first scientific environmental conference (2006) Zagazig University Egypt p. 49-65* – 2006

42. Slater M, Fisher C, – Electromagnetic field study. Effects of Electromagnetic Fields on Marine Species: a literature review – *Oregon Wave Energy Trust, 0905-00-001* – 1 September 2010

43. Shire GG, Brown K, Winegrad G - Communication towers: a deadly hazard to birds - *American Bird Conservancy, Washington DC USA, Special Report 230 species dead* – 2000

44. Jacobs N, NOAA - 5G Networks could throw weather forecasting into chaos – *Wired, Online, https://www.wired.com/story/5g-networks-could-throw-weather-forecasting-into-chaos/* – 17 May 2019

Consequences for the Earth

1. Pro Natura, Thielens A, Bell D, Mortimore DB, *et al.* - Exposure of Insects to high frequency EMF's from 2 to 120 GHz – *Ghent University Belgium, University of California Berkeley USA, University of Suffolk UK, Newbourne Solutions Ltd Woodbridge UK. Charles Sturt University Australia, Scientific Reports (2018) 8:3924, DOI:10.1038/s41598-018-22271-3* - 2 March 2018

2. Romanenko S, Begley R, Harvey AR, Hool L, *et al.* - The interaction between electromagnetic fields at MHz, GHz and THz frequencies with cells, tissues and organisms: risks and potential – *University of Western Australia, Perth, J.R.Soc.Interface, DOI:10.1098/rsif.2017.0585* - 14 August 2017

3. Feldman YD, Puzenko A, Ben Ishai P, Caduff A, *et al.* - Human skin as arrays of helical antennas in the millimeter and submillimeter wave range – *The Hebrew University Jerusalem and Ariel University, both in Israel, DOI:10.1103/PhysRevLett.100.128102* – 27 March 2018

4. Volland H – Book: Handbook of atmospheric electrodynamics - *526 Pages, ISBN 9781138559028* - 1995

5. Cherry N – EMF/EMR Reduces melatonin in animals and people - *Human Sciences Department, Lincoln University Canterbury, New Zealand* – 2 September 2001

Consequences for Humans

I Heart and blood vessels

1. Nguyen THP, Pham VTH, Baulin V, Croft RJ, *et al.* - The effect of a high frequency electromagnetic field in the microwave range on red blood cells – *Scientific Reports 7:10798 DOI:10.1038/s41598-017-11288-9* – 7 September 2017

2. Falcioni L, Bua L, Tibaldi E, *et al.* - Report of final results regarding brain and heart tumors in Sprague-Dawley rats exposed from prenatal life until natural death to mobile phone radiofrequency field representative of a 1.8GHz GSM base station environmental emission – 2018

3. Havas M - Radiation from wireless technology affects the blood, the heart, and the autonomic nervous system - *Rev.Environ.Health. p. 75-84* – 28 November 2013

4. Huber R, Schuderer J, Graf T, Jutz K, Borbely AA, Kuster N, Achermann P - Radio frequency electromagnetic field exposure in humans: Estimation of SAR distribution in the brain, effects on sleep and heart rate - *Bioelectromagnetics 24(4): p.262-276* – 2003

5. Jauchem JR, Ryan KL, Freidagger MR - Cardiovascular and thermal effects of microwave irradiation at 1 and/or 10 GHz in anesthetized rats - *Bioelectromagnetics 21(3): p.159-66* – 2000

6. Hocking B, Gordon I - Decreased survival for childhood leukaemia in proximity to TV towers - *Annual Scientific Meeting of the Royal Australasian College of Physicians in Adelaide, SA, 2-5* – May 2000

7. Michelozzi P, Ancona C, Fusco D, Forastiere F, Perucci CA - Risk of leukaemia and residence near a radio transmitter in Italy - *Epidemiology 9 (Suppl) 354p* – 1998

8. McKenzie DR, Yin Y, Morrell S - Childhood incidence of acute lymhoblastic leukaemia and exposure to broadcast radiation in Sydney, a second look – *Aust.NZ.J.Pub.Health 22 (3): p. 360-367* -1998

9. Szmigielski S, Bortkiewicz A, Gadzicka E, Zmyslony M, Kubacki R - Alteration of diurnal rhythms of blood pressure and heart rate to workers exposed to radiofrequency electromagnetic fields - *Blood Press Monit 3(6): p.323-330* – 1998

10. Bortkiewicz A, Gadzicka E, Zmyslony M - Heart rate variability in workers exposed to medium-frequency electromagnetic fields – *Nerv.Syst. 59(3): p. 91-97* – 1996

11. Maskarinec G, Cooper J, Swygert L - Investigation of increased incidence in childhood leukaemia near radio towers in Hawaii – *J.Environ.Pathol.Toxicol.Oncol. 13(1), 33-37* – 1994

I Head and nervous system

1. Ramazinni Institute - The Ramazzini Study. Increase in brain tumors with long term cell phone use over 10 years. This longitudinal NTP data supports 2 other scientific studies. – March 2018

2. Miller AB, Morgan LL, Udasin I, Davis DL – Increased risk of brain, vestibular nerve and salivary gland tumors are associated with mobile phone use. Nine studies (2011–2017) report increased risk of brain cancer from mobile phone use. Four case-control studies (3 in 2013, 1 in 2014) report increased risk of vestibular nerve tumors. Concern for other cancers: breast (male & female), testis, leukaemia, and thyroid - 6 September 2018

3. Zhang X, Huang WJ, Chen WW - Microwaves and Alzheimer's disease – *Exp.Ther.Med.; 12: p.1969–1972* – 2016

4. Medeiros LN, Sanchez TG - Tinnitus and cell phones: the role of electromagnetic radiofrequency radiation - *Braz J Otorhinolaryngol.;82(1):97, DOI:10.1016/j.bjorl.2015.04.013* – February 2016

5. Morgan LL, Miller AB, Sasco A, Davis DL - Mobile phone radiation causes brain tumors and should be classified as a probable human carcinogen - 25 February 2015

6. Schmid MR, Loughran SP, Regel SJ, *et al.* - Sleep EEG alterations: effects of different pulse-modulated radio frequency electromagnetic fields - *J Sleep Res 2012; 21: p. 50–58* – 2012

7. Ozdemir F, Kargi A - Electromagnetic Waves and Human Health. Epidemiologic evidence compiled in the period 2000-2010 starts to indicate an increased risk, in particular for brain tumors, from mobile phone use - *ISBN: 978-953-307-304-0, DOI:10.5772/16343* – 9 October 2010

8. Davanipour Z, Sobel E - Long-term exposure to magnetic fields and the risks of Alzheimer's disease and breast cancer - *Pathophysiology 16: p. 149-156* – 2009

9. Hardell L, Mild KH, Sandström M, Carlberg M, Hallquist A, Pahlson A - Vestibular schwannoma, tinnitus and cellular telephones - *Neuroepidemiol 22: p.124-129* – March 2003

I Immune system

1. Mina D, Sagonas K, Fragopoulou AF, Pafilis P, Skouroliakou A, Margaritis LH, *et al.* - Immune responses of a wall lizard to wholebody exposure to radiofrequency electromagnetic radiation - *International Journal of Radiation Biology, 92: p. 162–168. DOI:10.3109/09553002.2016.1135262* - 2016

2. Boscolo P, Raffaele Iovene R, Paiardini G - Electromagnetic fields and autoimmune diseases – *p. 79–83, ISSN: 2240-2594* – February 2014

3. Szmigielski S - Reaction of the immune system to low-level RF/MW exposures – *Sci.Total.Environ.; p. 454-455:393-400* – 1 June 2013

4. Johansson O - Disturbance of the immune system by electromagnetic fields. A potentially underlying cause for cellular damage and tissue repair reduction which could lead to disease and impairment - *Pathophysiology 16: p.157-177* – 23 April 2009

5. Lushnikov KV, Gapeev AB, Sadovnikov VB, Cheremis NK - Effect of extremely high frequency electromagnetic radiation of low intensity on parameters of humoral immunity in healthy mice - *Biofizika 46(4): p.753-760* - 2001
6. Fesenko EE, Makar VR, Novoselova EG, Sadovnikov VB - Microwaves and cellular immunity I & II Effect of whole body microwave irradiation on tumor necrosis factor production in mouse cells - *Bioelectrochem Bioenerg 49(1): p.29-35 & p.37-41* - 1999
7. Dmoch A, Moszczynski P - Levels of immunoglobulin and subpopulations of T lymphocytes and NK cells in men occupationally exposed to microwave radiation in frequencies of 6-12 GHz – *Med.Pr. 49(1): p.45-49* – 1998

I Bone system
1. Kunt H, Şentürk I, Gönül Y, Korkmaz M, Ahsen A, *et al.* - Effects of electromagnetic radiation exposure on bone mineral density, thyroid, and oxidative stress index in electrical workers – *Dovepress, Onco Targets and Therapy 2016:9 p.745-754, https://doi.org/10.2147/OTT.S94374* – 12 February 2016

I Mind, emotions and mental state
1. Foerster M - A Prospective Cohort Study of Adolescents Memory Performance and Individual Brain Dose of Microwave Radiation from Wireless Communication - *Environmental Health Perspectives 126 (7)* – 7 July 2018
2. Pall ML - Microwave frequency electromagnetic fields (EMFs) produce widespread neuropsychiatric effects including depression – *J.Chem.Neuroanat.;75(Pt B):43-51. DOI:10.1016/j.jchemneu* – September 2016
3. Hung CS, Anderson C, Horne JA, McEvoy P - Mobile phone 'talk-mode' signal delays EEG-determined sleep onset – *Neurosci.Lett. 421: p.82-86* – 2007
4. Hutter HP, Moshammer H, Wallner P, Kundi M - Subjective symptoms, sleeping problems, and cognitive performance in subjects living near mobile phone base stations – *Occup.Environ.Med. 63(5): p. 307-313* – 2006
5. Loughran SP, Wood AW, Barton JM, Croft RJ, Thompson B, Stough C - The effect of electromagnetic fields emitted by mobile phones on human sleep - *Neuroreport. 16(17): p.1973-1976* – 2005
6. Al-Khlaiwi T, Meo SA - Association of mobile phone radiation with fatigue, headache, dizziness, tension and sleep disturbance in Saudi population - *Saudi Med.J. 25(6):732-736* – 2004
7. Bortkiewicz, *et al.* - Residents close to mobile phone masts report more incidences of circulatory problems, sleep disturbances, irritability, depression, blurred vision, and concentration difficulties the nearer they live to the mast – 2004
8. Santini R, Santini P, Le Ruz P, Danze JM, Seigne M - Survey study of people living in the vicinity of cellular phone base stations – *Electromag.Biol.Med. 22: p. 41-49* – 2003
9. Santini R, Santini P, Danze JM, Le Ruz P - Study of the health of people living in the vicinity of mobile phone base stations: I. Influence of distance and sex – *Pathol.Biol. 50(6): p. 369-373* – 2002
10. Huber R, Graf T, Gallmann E, Matter D, Wittmann L, Schuderer J, Kuster N, Borbely AA, Achermann P - Exposure to pulsed high-frequency electromagnetic field during waking affects human sleep EEG – *NeuroReport, volume 11, number 15, p. 3321-3325* - 2000
11. Huber R, Treyer V, Borbély AA, Buck A, Achermann PJ, Schuderer J, Gottselig JM, Landolt H-P, Werth E, Berthold T, Kuster N - Electromagnetic fields, such as those from mobile phones, alter regional cerebral blood flow and sleep and waking EEG – *P.J.Sleep.Res. 11: p.289-295* – 2002
12. Hamblin DL, Wood AW - Effects of mobile phone emissions on human brain activity and sleep variables – *Int.J.Radiat.Biol. 78(8): p.659-669* – 2002

13. Lebedeva NN, Sulimov AV, Sulimova OP, Korotkovskaya TI, Gailus T - Investigation of brain potentials in sleeping humans exposed to the electromagnetic field of mobile phones – *Crit.Rev.Biomed.Eng. 29(1): p. 125-133* – 2001
14. Wijngaarden E van, David A, Savitz, Kleckner RC, Cai J, Loomis D - Exposure to electromagnetic fields and suicide among electric utility workers; a nested case-control study – *West.J.Med.; 173(2): p. 94–100, DOI:10.1136/ewjm.173.2.94* – August 2000
15. Borbely AA, Huber R, Gallmann E, Achermann P, Graf T, Fuchs B - Pulsed high-frequency electromagnetic field affects human sleep and sleep electroencephalogram – *Neurosci.Lett. 275(3): p.207-210* – 1999
16. Kolodynski, Kolodynska - School children living near a radio location station in Latvia suffered reduced motor function, memory and attention spans – *Sci.Total.Environ. 180(1): p.87-93* – 1999

I Sperm cells and egg cells

1. Tirpak F, Slanina T, Tomka M, Zidek R, Halo M, Ivanic P, Gren A, Formicki G, Lukac N, Massanyi P - Exposure to non-ionizing electromagnetic radiation of public risk prevention instruments threatens the quality of spermatozoids (bovine spermatozoa research) – *Reproduction in Domestic Animals, volume 54, issue 2, p. 150-159, https://doi.org/10.1111/rda.13338* – 7 September 2018
2. Houston BJ, Nixon B, King BV, Aitken RJ, De Iuliis GN - The effects of radiofrequency electromagnetic radiation on sperm function – *Reproduction; volume 152, issue 6, p. R263– R276, https://doi.org/10.1530/REP-16-0126* - 2016
3. Zalata A, El-Samanoudy A, Shaalan D, El-Baiomy Y, Ayman MD, Mostafa T - Effect of Cell Phone Radiation on Motility, DNA Fragmentation and Clusterin Gene Expression in Human Sperm – *Int.J.Fertil.Steril.; 9(1): p. 129–136, DOI:10.22074/ijfs.2015.4217* – April-June 2015
4. Adams JA, Galloway TS, Mondal D, Esteves SC - Effect of mobile telephones on sperm quality: A systematic review and meta-analysis - *University of Exeter UK, Environment.Int. 70, p. 106-112, DOI:10.1016/j.envint.2014.04.015* - 2014
5. Kibona L - Assessment of the impact of EM radiations from mobile phone towers on male sperm infertility - *Ruaha University College Tanzania, International Journal of Technology enhancement and emerging engineering Research, volume 1, issue 4, ISSN 2347-4289* - 2013
6. Özorak A, Nazıroğlu M, Çelik Ö, Yüksel M, Özçelik D, Özkaya MO, Çetin H, Kahya MC, Kose SA - Wifi (2.45 GHz) and mobile phone (900 and 1800 MHz) induced risks on oxidative stress and elements in kidney and testis of rats during pregnancy and the development of offspring - *Biol Trace Elem Res.;156(1-3):221-9. DOI:10.1007/s12011-013-9836-z* – December 2013
7. Li DK, Chen H, Odouli R - Maternal exposure to magnetic fields during pregnancy in relation to the risk of asthma in offspring – *Arch.Pediatr.Adolesc.Med.;165(10): p. 945-50. DOI:10.1001/archpediatrics.2011.135* – October 2011
8. Han J, Cao Z, Liu X, Zhang W - Effect of early pregnancy electromagnetic field exposure on embryo growth ceasing - *Wei Sheng Yan Jiu (Journal of Hygiene Research);39(3): p. 349-352* – May 2010

I Derailment of cell growth

1. Hertsgaard M, Dowie M – The inconvenient truth about cancer and mobile phones – *The Guardian Online: https://www.theguardian.com/technology/2018/jul/14/mobile-phones-cancer-inconvenient-truths* - 14 July 2018
2. Meijer DKF, Geesink JH - Favourable and unfavourable EMF frequency patterns in Cancer - *University of Groningen and Biophysics Group Loon op Zand NL*– 12 March 2018
3. Blask D, Eberle S, Golomb B, Marachi R - Physicians for safe technology, NTP Study on cell Phones and Cancer; clear evidence of carcinogenicity – 2 February 2018
4. Markov MS, Pall ML - How cancer can be caused by microwave frequency electromagnetic field (EMF) exposures: EMF activation of voltage-gated calcium channels (VGCCs) can cause

cancer including tumor promotion, tissue invasion and metastasis via 15 mechanisms - *Taylor & Francis Group, Online; https://www.taylorfrancis.com/books/e/9780203705100/chapters/10.1201/b22486-7* - 2018

5. Havas M - When theory and observation collide: Can non-ionizing radiation cause cancer? – *Environ. Pollut. 2017;221:501-505, DOI:10.1016/j.envpol.2016.10.018* – October 2016

6. Havas M - Carcinogenic effects of Non-Ionizing Radiation: A Paradigm Shift - *Trent University, Canada, JSM Environ.Sci.Ecol. 5(2): 1045* – 2 June 2017

7. Pall ML – Book: On 5G – *Online available: https://www.emfacts.com/2018/08/martin-palls-book-on-5g-is-available-online/* – 2018

8. Mahdavi M, Yekta R, Tackallou SH - Positive correlation between ELF and RF electromagnetic fields on cancer risk – *University of Tabriz Iran and Islamic Azad University of Tehran Iran, Journal of Paramedical Sciences, volume 6, number 3, ISSN 2008-4978* - 2015

9. Dode AC, Leão MM, Tejo Fde A, Gomes AC, Dode DC, Dode MC, Moreira CW, Condessa VA, Albinatti C, Caiaffa WT - Mortality by neoplasia and cellular telephone base stations in the Belo Horizonte municipality, Minas Gerais state, Brazil - Direct link between 4.924 cancer deaths and cellular antenna radiation – *Sci.Total.Environ. 409(19):3649-3665, DOI:10.1016/j.scitotenv.2011.05.051*- 17 May 2011

10. Yakymenko I, Sidorik E, Kyrylenko S, Chekhun V - Long-term exposure to microwave radiation provokes cancer growth; evidences from radars and mobile communication systems - *R.E. Kavetsky Institute of Experimental Pathology, Oncology and Radiobiology of NAS of Ukraine, Exp.Oncol. volume 33, issue 2, p. 62-70* – June 2011

11. Elliott P, Toledano MB, Bennett J, de Hoogh BK, Best N, Briggs DJ - Mobile phone base stations and early childhood cancers - *Brit.Med.J., 340, p. 477* – 2010

12. Carpenter DO - Electromagnetic fields and cancer: the cost of doing nothing – *Rev.Environ.Health 25: p. 75-80* - 2010

13. West JG, Kapoor NS, Liao SY, Chen JW, Bailey L, Nagourney RA - Multifocal breast cancer in young women with prolonged contact between their breasts and their cellular phones - *DOI:10.1155/2013/354682* – 18 September 2013

14. Chen Q, Lang L, Wu W, Xu G, Zhang X, Li T, Huang H – A Meta-analysis on the relationship between exposure to ELF-EMFs and the risk of female breast cancer - *PLoS One. 2013; 8(7): e69272, DOI:10.1371/journal.pone.0069272* - 15 July 2013

15. Tynes T, Hannevik M, Anderson A, Vistnes AI, Haldorsen T - Incidence of breast cancer in Norwegian female radio and telegraph operators - *Cancer Registry of Norway, Cancer Causes Control 7(2):197-204* - 1996

16. Cantor KP, Stewart PA, Brinton LA, Dosemeci M - Occupational exposures and female breast cancer mortality in the United States – *J.Occup.Environ.Med. 1995 Mar;37(3):336-48, DOI:10.1097/00043764-199503000-00011* - 1995

I Autism

1. Herbert MR, Sage C - Autism and EMF? Plausibility of a pathophysiological link – *Elsevier Ltd, Research Program Neurology, Massachusetts General Hospital, Harvard Medical School, Boston USA, PMID: 24095003, DOI:10.1016/j.pathophys.2013.08.001* - 2013

I Metal bed springs

1. Hallberg Ö, Johansson O - Sleep on the right side. Get cancer on the left? - *Researchers of Hallberg Independent Research, the Karolinska Institute, both in Sweden – Journal Pathophysiology, volume 17, Issue 3 (June 2010), https://doi.org/10.1016/j.pathophys.2009.07.001* - 2 August 2010

I Future

1. Ali MA, Hekmat O, Aziza A, Elsayeda HM, et al - Effect of mobile phone radiation on proliferation and apoptosis in rabbit testes: a histological and immunohistochemical study - DOI:10.1097/01.EHX.0000473760.14176.a8 – December 2015

2. Zakharchenko MV, Kovzan AV, Khunderyakova NV, Yachkula TV, Krukova OV, Khlebopros RG, Shvartsburd PM, Fedotcheva NI, Litvinova EG, Kondrashova MN - The effect of cell-phone radiation on rabbits: Lymphocyte enzyme-activity data – Biophysics (2016) 61: 100, Pleiades Publishing https://doi.org/10.1134/S0006350916010279 – January 2016

3. Grigor'ev IuG, Luk'ianova SN, Makarov VP, Rynskov VV - Motor activity of rabbits in conditions of chronic low-intensity pulse microwave irradiation - Radiats Biol Radioecol. 1995 Jan-Feb;35(1):29-35 - PMID: 7719427 – January/ February 1995

4. Güler G, Tomruk A, Ozgur E, Sahin D, Sepici A, Altan N, Seyhan N – The effect of radiofrequency radiation on DNA and lipid damage in female and male infant rabbits - Gazi University, Ankara, Turkey, Int.J.Radiat.Biol. p. 367-373, PMID:22145622, DOI:10.3109/09553002.2012.646349 - April 2012

5. Shandala MG, Dumanskii UD, Rudnev MI, Ershova LK, Los IP - Study of nonionizing microwave radiation effects upon the central nervous system and behaviour reactions – Environ.Health Perspect. 30:p.115-121, PMID: 446442, DOI:10.1289/ehp.7930115 – June 1979

6. Kojima M, Hata I, Wake K, Watanabe S - Influence of anaesthesia on ocular effects and temperature in rabbit eyes exposed to microwaves - Bioelectromagnetics. (3):228-233, DOI:10.1002/bem.10195 – April 2004

7. Saili L, Hanini A, Smirani C, Azzouz A, Sakly M, Abdelmeek H, Boeslama Z - Effects of acute exposure to Wifi signals (2.45 GHz) on heart variability and blood pressure in Albinos rabbit – Elsevier Ltd. Environmental Toxicology and Pharmacology, volume 40, issue 2, p. 600-605, https://doi.org/10.1016/j.etap.2015.08.015 – September 2015

8. Marino AA, Frilot C, Nilsen E - Localization of electroreceptive function in rabbits – Elsevier Inc. Physiology & Behavior 79: p. 803-810, DOI:10.1016/S0031-9384(03)00206-3 – October 2003

9. Durgun M, Dasdag S, Erbatur S, Yegin K, Durgun SO, Uzun C, Ogucu G, Alabalik U, Akdag MZ - Effect of 2100 MHz mobile phone radiation on healing of mandibular fractures: an experimental study in rabbits - Biotechnology & Biotechnological Equipment 30(1):1-9, DOI:10.1080/13102818.2015.1102612 - 29 September 2015

10. Schaefer RK, Paxton LJ, Selby C, Ogorzalek B, Romeo G, Wolven B, Hsieh SY – Observation and modelling of the South Atlantic Anomaly in low Earth orbit using photometric instrument data - New maps of the south Atlantic anomaly, Space Weather, volume 14, issue 5, p. 330-342, John Hopkins University, https://doi.org/10.1002/2016SW001371 – September 2016

11. Wiseman R – Book: Quirkology: The curious science of everyday lives. International experiment proves pace of life is speeding op by 10 percent – University of Hertfordshire ISBN:0465090796 (ISBN13: 9780465090792) - 27 August 2007

Printed in Germany
by Amazon Distribution
GmbH, Leipzig